I'm Still Me

by
Joan Harper

Logos International
Plainfield, New Jersey

to Lisa

Foreword

It is my pleasure to introduce you to Joan Harper—a lovely lady whom the heavenly Father introduced to my wife and me about six years ago. Since that time, we've grown to know and love her as a woman who has tasted virtually every flavor of bitterness the human dilemma can deliver. The loveliest thing of all is that through everything, a fundamental sweetness in her personality has been preserved.

Now for some people, "sweet" may conjure up an image of the professional, superficial, pasted-on smile of a PR rep. In Joan, however, you are encountering a gracious, truly honest-to-God woman, whom God has enabled to handle pain and trial with the regal bearing of a queen. There is a Holy Spirit-begotten majesty in her life.

And one other thing.

Joan is a giver. My wife, Anna, and I agree that we have known few like Joan, whose life flows so unselfishly, springing from a well of commitment to the Spirit of God.

Like the gift-giving Spirit who indwells her, she is always disposed to minister lovingly and abundantly—whether of her time, her abilities or her personal resources. She isn't wealthy, but if she were a pauper she would find a way to give. Her sense of God's purpose in her life requires that of her.

She has written a book. It is about herself, but not for herself. You'll see what I mean, for you will shortly realize how much it was written for you. I happen to be mentioned in this story, but so are you. You'll find yourself between the lines, for in certain respects we have all experienced trials, tests and tragedies—but not always with such results.

Best of all, you will profit as you share in her discovering the pathway of true self-recovery in spite of anything—or everything.

Jack W. Hayford, Pastor
The Church on the Way
Van Nuys, California

Acknowledgments

I owe much to my Aunt Faith. True to her name, she has pointed me toward the path of faith more times than I can count. And it was she who first suggested I write a book.

Jean Dorman, Bernie Porter, and Nancy Southwell have been good friends. And like good friends, they pitched in to proofread and critique the manuscript, especially in its final stages. Their perspectives and acumen have been invaluable.

About midway into this job, I started looking about for a typist. I found Kathy Zander. But Kathy turned out to be much more than a typist. Kathy's help proved invaluable in rewriting the closing chapters. Her typing is good, and her skill in writing is remarkable.

I made a new friend while writing this story. Through publishing circles I was introduced to Dennis Baker, who agreed to be my editor and co-worker. At the outset I hoped he would write the book for me, but he refused. Instead, he told me I could do it with a little help and he proceeded to make me work hard. I had to think deeply about my life. I had to deal with complex emotions. Worse, I had to be honest. And Dennis's sensitivity and ability to express his insights have kept me honest. He was being a friend and I love him for it.

Not far from my home, on a hillside, stands an old oak tree. About a year ago, a photographer and a graphics man carefully carved a heart in the tree with the words, "Jesus and me." They took a picture of it and used it for a magazine. Now I use that tree as a special place to visit God.

One day not long ago I strolled up the hillside to visit the tree and spend some time—just Jesus and me. Beneath the oak's sturdy branches, I felt an increasing sense of humility before the God who had created this majestic tree. I was praying, and yet the words seemed so empty, so futile, so inadequate. How do you talk to such a great God? Just from the heart. He knows our hearts, better than we do.

I was thinking that day about the many scars on my body—the accidents and operations. What did they mean? I was tempted to feel sorry for myself, but I was reminded of a couplet I read somewhere:

For what are trivial things like scars
To one who shares the night with stars?

1

January 1972. Richard Nixon was perched on the brink of his second election year. I was perched on the brink of my second half. Before the month was out, I would be forty. Some people say life begins at forty. Maybe, I thought.

I was still going to the psychiatrist. He was someone I could talk to. My husband, Arnold, had come with me for several weeks late in 1971, but he grew weary of it and stopped. Life was bleak and I was no longer a youngster.

One evening shortly after my birthday, I was lying in bed reading a magazine article about cancer. Los Angeles was having one of its infrequent electrical storms. The sky was rumbling. I laid my hand on my right breast, checking for a telltale lump. Suddenly my hand froze. There were no lumps, but I knew I had cancer. A cold terror enveloped me. I was utterly alone with my knowledge.

I spent two months trying to talk myself out of it. Finally I went to my gynecologist and asked for an exam. He complied and then assured me everything was in order. No signs of cancer.

"Look, Joni," he cleared his throat, "you seem fine to me. It's good to be on the alert for this kind of thing, but don't let it develop into a cancerphobia. You seem awfully intense about this. Do you think it has anything to do with your mother? She had her mastectomy less than three years ago."

"This isn't a phobia, Harold. I knew what you might think—what anyone might think. You're the first person I've mentioned it to for just that reason. I haven't even told my psychiatrist. I know how it sounds, but I have this mysterious certainty."

"Joan, I'm sorry. All I can tell you for sure is that there's no sign of breast cancer from my examination."

I tried doubly hard to talk myself out of it after that. I had by this time compiled a sizeable file of articles about breast cancer. I had read everything I could lay my hands on. I knew the facts. Maybe I *was* crazy. But none of the facts made any difference. I knew I had cancer.

By the end of the next month, I had made an appointment with a radiologist for a mammogram. I trembled as the day approached. I knew, and yet I didn't want to know.

The day dawned gloomy and rainy. I didn't want to go. My certainty and urgency had vanished. Now I was telling myself how foolish I'd been to waste three months of my life fretting over something that didn't exist. I picked up the phone to cancel the appointment. "Don't do it. Put the phone down and go." The voice was almost audible. I obeyed.

"Joni, I can't find anything to make me suspect you have breast cancer. I'll do the mammography, but just to set your mind at ease. I'm doing it as a favor, not because I think it's advisable." Dr. Rodgers couldn't quite conceal his exasperation. Afterwards, as he was escorting me out of his office, he promised he would call Arnold at the office as soon as he got the results.

The next morning I called Dr. Rodgers's office myself. His nurse said the results would be in later in the day. Part of me wanted to believe everything was all right, so I went about my business and tried not to think about it too much. When by the end of the day I still had heard nothing, I wasn't alarmed. No news was good news, I decided, and didn't call back.

I was in the kitchen fixing dinner when Arnold came home from the office earlier than usual. I turned as he came through the kitchen door. He looked devastated. He embraced me anxiously and blurted out, "You've got cancer. My God, Joni, you've got cancer!"

I froze for an instant and then began to weep. "Lord, not yet, it's too soon. I've got a daughter to raise. I don't want to die!"

How often had I wanted to die? But I didn't think of that then. I got dizzy and saw flashing lights. I grabbed the back of a chair and Arnold led me into the living room to sit down.

"There are definite signs of cancer in the right breast, Joni," Arnold said somberly, dropping his voice so Lisa would not hear him. "It just doesn't figure—you're totally free of any lumps or symptoms."

"What am I going to do?"

"The first thing is to call Dr. Marks," he said, just as

3

Lisa walked into the room.

"Mommy, why are you crying?" She came over and put her arms around me.

"Mommy doesn't feel well tonight. Why don't you and I help her get dinner on the table?"

I wondered how and when we would tell Lisa and how she would handle the situation. Then I told myself I had to pull myself together and not let my dread show through. My stomach was tied up in knots, but I breezed through dinner and marveled afterwards at my ability to deny my feelings. And now, I thought, the hurt and the rage, the fears and the sorrows I had clutched to myself all these years had taken on a life of their own and I had cancer.

We called Dr. Marks, a well-known surgeon in the San Fernando Valley. He was to call us as soon as he got home. When the telephone rang, it startled me. "I'll get it!" I snapped at Arnold. But he already had the receiver. Shortly he said, "Dick wants to talk to you, honey."

"Now, what's all the excitement about, Joni?" I told him my version of the events and then he asked me to come into his office the next afternoon for an examination.

"Oftentimes a mammogram is erroneous. I've seen many that looked like cancer on film and the biopsy showed nothing, or a benign tumor. So let's not get too worried, okay?"

"Okay," I agreed with my mouth, but I felt he was being patronizing and it irritated me.

After examining me and the mammogram, Dick said, "I'm going to call the hospital right now. I want you in there tomorrow for a biopsy of the right breast."

"I need one more day," I said. "I have to make arrangements for Lisa, and I have a couple of things at the

4

office to take care of."

He frowned. "Okay, but the next day for sure."

"All right. But if you find cancer, I don't want to wake up without a breast."

"I promise, Joan. A biopsy, nothing more—no matter what."

Thursday afternoon Arnold drove me to the hospital. As I slowly walked down the corridor, a chilling horror came over me, like a net from which I could not escape.

I awakened Friday afternoon. My breast burned with pain. Groggily, I started tugging at my nightgown.

"No, no, Joni, it's all right—wake up! You've had a biopsy. Remember?" It was Arnold.

"Is it cancerous?"

"We don't know yet. They'll let us know in a couple of days. The report can't be gotten out with the weekend and all."

That was strange. I knew a pathologist could evaluate a frozen section in a matter of a few minutes. And yet, here we were, waiting several days—I felt as if everything was okay. After knowing for more than three months that I had cancer, fear caused me to deny anything was wrong.

Saturday afternoon, after I had gotten home from the hospital, my dad came to visit. He was acting rather peculiarly. Come to think of it, so was Arnold, but I chalked it up to the agony of waiting and the strain of not knowing. Dr. Marks's reason for the delay was that he wanted to send the tissue studies to several pathologists for comparison. I bought his story—too easily—and told one of the women at work I'd be back the following Monday.

Tuesday afternoon Dr. Marks finally called.

"Joni, I'd like to see you in my office later this

afternoon, around five o'clock." His voice sounded grave.

"I'm going to have to have a breast removed, aren't I?"

"That's not entirely the picture. Let's just wait until this afternoon—we'll talk then."

Great sobs welled up within me and I wanted to scream. I decided not to call Arnold. I got ready for the appointment and then called my Aunt Faith to tell her how fearful I was. She began to pray, and the only thing I really heard her say was, "Lord, give her peace and composure now." I tried to look composed as I walked into Dick's office.

He greeted me. "I've called Arnold and he should be here in a few minutes. I want to discuss this with both of you." I began to tremble and thought I would faint. We waited about ten minutes and then Dick called me in. "I guess Arnold has been detained. Let's go ahead without him."

He looked at me with compassion and sorrow. "Joni, we are going to have to remove both breasts."

"My God, no! Why?" I put my face in my hands and wept as if I would never stop.

2

Where had it all begun? I felt as if I'd always struggled to survive, even when we lived in the large, two-story house on Burt Street in Omaha, Nebraska.

Memories of that house always bring to mind the white snow of my ninth winter, the glistening silver of the moon upon it—and the crimson blood, a trail of it: my mother's blood.

My parents were out the night before and had an argument as they were coming into the house. The next morning mom appeared with a black eye and a swollen lip.

"Joan, you and Larry go out and look for my glasses. They fell off in the front yard when dad hit me," she explained simply.

They were easy to find because of the trail of blood across the crisp snow. This little task I could do for my mother seemed to still some of the hurt and rage I felt, and the resentment that seethed against my dad. I knew why he had hit her. I'd heard him do it before. It was when he'd come home from a night out without her.

"Dean, is that you?" It was my mother's voice and she hadn't sounded happy.

"Yeah." Dad's voice had been sullen.

"Where have you been?"

"What do you care?"

"You've been drinking again, haven't you?"

"Shut up! It's no worse than you taking all those damn pills and sleeping all day."

"I hate it when you drink. How much money did you leave at that bar?"

"Look who's worried about money all of a sudden, the original good-time Charlie of Burt Street! You spend it faster than I can bring it home."

"You liar! You never were anything but a no-good shanty Irishman!"

"Why you little bear cat, I'll teach you to call me that!"

There was a sickening slap, and then my mother's tears could be heard from where my brother and I lay stone still in our beds.

I used to burn when dad hit mom. She was a little person. She never had a chance to defend herself. One time I wasn't in bed. Mom and dad were having a fight at the kitchen table. Just as he was shouting some threat at my mother, I picked up my iced tea glass and hurled its contents, ice and all, right into his face. Then I ran for my life. But he finally caught me and then I had bruises just like my mom's.

It seemed to me I got more than my share of "good old-fashioned" beatings, and I recall the confusion I felt because I had not really done anything "bad." Once when I was five, I was told to watch my baby brother in the back yard. I was easily distracted, and Larry somehow got to the front, near the street. Dad came home, went into a rage, dragged me into the house and gave me a terrific spanking. I was so black and blue I could not sit for days.

It was not long before I began to feel guilty and think there must be something wrong with me. Why did mom and dad get so angry with me? What was there about me they didn't love?

As I grew older, mom had fits of depression that were difficult for her to cope with. Along with chronic headaches and frequent illnesses, she was irritable and lost her temper often, sometimes going into a rage that terrified me. It seemed to me I was the focus of her anger much more so than my brother, and this intensified my feelings of inadequacy. I began to work harder and harder, trying to do something to make my parents love and recognize me. This was to be the pattern of my life for about forty years.

When I was twelve, my parents moved to Colorado but allowed me to stay in Omaha to finish out the school year. I lived with a family named Love—and loving they were. Their daughter Lorraine was my best friend and her parents treated me as their own. But I missed my parents, and looked forward to the day they would come back to attend my confirmation ceremony. Mom sent me a pretty gold cross, but they didn't make the trip back as they had neither the "time nor the money." We had our pictures taken that day, and the shutter snapped just as I was licking a big tear off my cheek.

A few months after I rejoined my family, we moved back to Omaha just in time for me to be enrolled in North High School. I was just beginning to feel at home there when one day my dad walked into my classroom and spoke to my teacher. As I met dad outside in the hall, he said, "Get your things together, we're leaving for California." I was perplexed and unhappy. I'll never know how they had gotten all packed up in one day, but we were off to California before the day was out.

I was determined, however, to live in Omaha, and without thinking of the consequences, I left our motel room in Laramie, Wyoming, at five in the morning and started down the highway. I had only a sweater to keep me warm and about four dollars in my purse. But I knew we were getting closer to California and it was now or never!

After walking awhile, I was cold and hungry. The traffic began to pick up so I walked on the side of the road in the weeds that screened me somewhat from view. Shortly a police car pulled up. My dad was in it.

"Kind of cold for an early morning walk, isn't it, kid?" dad said. *Kind* of cold? I thought. I'm freezing! I wondered what the policemen were going to do to me.

"We found a young girl down here in this very same culvert just last week," one of the policemen said. "She had been attacked and beaten. It would be a good idea if you just stuck with your parents." That was all, but the message hit home as I realized what a foolish thing I had done.

"Come on, kid, let's go get some hot chocolate and a doughnut," my dad said. He told me things would be better for me once we got settled in California. "Don't worry so much, it'll all work out."

My parents found a little home in West Los Angeles. The house was very small, having only two tiny bedrooms, but mom wanted it.

"It's just a cute little dollhouse and I know I can fix it up to look real adorable. Please, Dean?"

That was it; the house was theirs. One problem remained: there was not enough room for all of us. My folks talked to Aunt Faith, who with my grandmother had preceded us to California one year earlier. They all agreed I would go to Monrovia and live with them for a while. Then they came and told me.

"No room for me," I thought. "What about Larry—why can't he go live with someone else? Why do I have to be the one to leave home?" Maybe mom was still angry with me for trying to run away that time in Laramie.

"How could you have done such a stupid thing?" she had screamed. "I could just kill you for doing this to us, you stupid little brat!" My heart still hurt when I remembered.

"Mom, are you still mad at me? Is that why you don't want me?"

"It isn't that I don't want you. Larry is just too young."

"Besides," dad added, "it won't be for long. Soon we'll get on our feet again and buy a larger house and you can come home."

I lay awake that first night in Monrovia weeping, looking back over the last few years. Why, I asked myself, was I such a creep that even my own parents didn't want me?

As I began to settle in with Aunt Faith and Uncle Gene, I could not help but notice how much happier they were than my parents. They both made a fuss over me and showed me a great deal of love.

"I've always wanted a daughter," Aunt Faith said. "Now I have you—you'll be just like my very own."

Gene's favorite way of showing his feelings was to tease

or play a joke on me. We'd laugh and laugh, teasing and chasing one another, until Aunt Faith would say, "I don't know what I'm going to do with you two kids. Settle down!"

I loved going to their Episcopal church on Sunday mornings. Kneeling and praying and singing to God pleased me. I would leave church light-heartedly. Life seemed good again. I was not prepared for what happened after I had been with them only eight short months.

When I returned home from school one day Aunt Faith said, "Your mom and dad are coming out for you next weekend. They are converting the garage into a room for Larry, and they want you to come home." Home? I thought; this is home. I left in tears.

Things were worse than ever at home. I often asked myself, How can I get out of here? Where can I go? Who would want me? I was enrolled in Hamilton High and found it difficult to make friends. I felt intimidated and estranged, and began to protect myself by being aloof. During the lunch breaks I was afraid to be alone in the crowd and I would take my lunch into the restroom and hide in a cubicle to eat.

Finally a girl named Barbara asked me point-blank: "How come you're so snooty—what makes you so special?" I burst into tears.

"I don't feel special. I feel afraid and lonely!"

The mask was off and Barbara and I began a warm friendship. She was close to another gal named Betsy and the three of us became nearly inseparable. We all had nice legs and were dubbed "the girls with the gams."

I began to work after school for our physician, Dr. Paskan—filing, running errands, cleaning, helping out with all sorts of things—whatever he or his nurses asked me to do. I went all out to please everyone there. I liked being a part of a business that was helping people, and my instinctive sympathy for people who were ill came readily to the fore.

Over the years Dr. Paskan was to patiently teach me all phases of medical assisting and medical management. Often he would ask me to consider a professional career.

"You are a good diagnostician and have some darn good business acumen. You ought to think of becoming a doctor." I was impressed, but never seriously considered medical school. I didn't think I was good enough or smart enough.

Besides, a career with Dr. Paskan was all the future I dreamed of. The pride he took in his work rubbed off on all of us, but it was his stature in my eyes as a man that gradually narrowed my interests in other men, and in other goals. He was a girl's dream come to life, a handsome man with an intense yet gentle nature. He gave of himself easily to others. When he flashed that beautiful smile at me—made all the whiter by a skiing tan—his good looks radiated a warm humor and a zest for living that were contagious. As I grew from a fourteen-year-old girl to a nineteen-year-old woman in his world, I came to feel I was an excellent candidate for ending his thirty-odd years of bachelorhood. I was young, but I was fast becoming a very pretty lady. And yet, I was only one among many, as his passion for skiing was rivaled by his interest in beautiful women.

So after high school I was quite content to work long hours, and since mom did not want me to go away to nursing school, I took a class here and there. I spent the rest of my time studying music.

Dr. Paskan had noticed my interest in music, and he began to foster it—he was always looking after my best interests.

"Remember the new patient I made a house call on the other day?" he asked me one lunch hour when he'd come upon me poring over the libretto of an opera I'd seen the night before. I nodded.

"Well, just guess who he is—Maestro Leon Cepparo, vocal coach for some of the singing stars at MGM, soon to be Joan Hurley's vocal coach. You, young lady, are going to be in show biz!"

As I left the office that warm August evening, a Santa Ana breeze, balmy and soft, was blowing through my hair and my heart was singing. The next day I would be interviewed by the incomparable Maestro Cepparo! I dreamed of becoming a great singing star. "I'll be good and I'll be rich and famous. I'll make a name for myself and mom and dad will really be proud of me."

The next day I arrived at the old Culver Mansion and while I waited in the drawing room for Maestro to finish the lesson he was giving, my heart pounded. The strains of a beautiful aria drifted through the room: "O, mio babbino caro. . . ." I dreamed of what it would be like to sing those words.

The interview commenced, and up and down the scale we went, my nervous lyric soprano voice trilling away, "La, la, la, la, la."

"Yes, yes, I think you have it, my dear. I should like to take you under my wing. And with that face and those beautiful blue eyes, you should be a big hit once you have full control of your voice."

I was thrilled! We decided that lessons twice a week would be best, but I did not have the money. Maestro said, "Not to worry, you can repay me when you're a star. For now we will do it for half price."

After a few months I ventured out into some solo work in the church choir and at some weddings. When I was singing, I felt bathed in a warm glow; the fear, pain and aloneness of the past would drop off like fall leaves in a windstorm. The message of the song would sink into my inmost self, and I would live in the world it described. I could be someone else for those moments.

One Saturday afternoon, Maestro looked at me with a twinkle in his eye. "You're about to learn a lovely new aria. I hope you like it." He put his hands on the keyboard and the enchanting strains of "O, Mio Babbino Caro" wafted across the room.

"Do you really think I can sing that?" I squealed.

"Let's give it a try."

Try I did, and to me it was beautiful!

"Hello there, what have we here? Hold your head back a moment, please—hmm." Dr. Vincent was minding the office while Dr. Paskan was on vacation. For several months I had been losing weight and becoming unusually nervous and high-strung. Dr. Vincent had said, "You're too damned skinny. Don't you eat anything?" and I had thrown my head back in laughter. I had an enormous appetite—for a girl, I had always been told. That was when he noticed the enlargement in my neck.

"I think you'd better go see a specialist," he said. "I could run some tests on you, Joni, but you'd still need another physician. Might as well just let him do it all."

I was frightened and ran to the mirror to take a look at my neck. "What do you think is wrong with me? Is it a thyroid problem?"

"I'm afraid so—wait and see."

He sent me to a doctor in Beverly Hills. I was quite agitated and on the verge of tears all the way to his office. Dr. Baumgartner was a kind-looking, grey-haired gentleman who immediately put me at ease. However, the seriousness with which he examined me was alarming.

"What's wrong with me, doctor?"

"Well, my dear, that is what we are about to find out." He made another appointment for me to have some blood tests and a basal metabolism test in the next day or two; the results brought bad news.

"You have a thyroid problem that is going to require surgery." I looked at him as if I didn't know whether to believe him or not, and he added gravely, "It's serious."

"What about my singing? Will surgery affect my voice?"

"You'll feel better than ever after this surgery—don't worry about your voice."

It was a beautiful May day and I was wishing I didn't have to leave when mom said, "Come on, Joan, we can't wait any longer, we've got to leave for the hospital." My tension was at an all time high. I wondered what it would be like to die. Would anyone miss me? Would I go to heaven? Hell? If I didn't die, could I still work towards a career in opera? I didn't like not having the answers to these questions.

I awakened violently ill and in much pain. It seems I had awakened earlier complaining of pain and they had given me an injection of morphine. As we were soon to discover,

I had an allergy to that and to several other medications. Aunt Faith and mom were both there and told me I had been in surgery for over three hours. Later the doctor told me the goiter had wrapped itself around my windpipe.

"It was a more complicated surgery than we had expected. No wonder you were so nervous. That thing was quite large and pouring toxins into your system. You're going to be a different young lady now. I think you'll like yourself a little more and have a better outlook on life."

My recovery took some time and I rather enjoyed all the fuss everyone was making over me, especially the urging to gain a little weight. I didn't need to be asked twice to tie into some homemade goody. I was alive and apparently well, and eagerly anticipating my return to my music lessons. Finally Dr. Baumgartner said it would be all right to use my voice and promised to come to my first concert.

With my dreams intact, I went back to studying music. At first we thought the change in my voice would be temporary—I was just a little "rusty." Also, I was having some allergy problems and a sinus condition that had come and gone since my tonsillectomy a couple of years before, but I was attributing this to the summer weather. As time went on the problem grew. Maestro suggested I try different music as my voice was quite a bit lower. I took his suggestion and had one of my own. Why not redouble my efforts? Maybe it's like starting over again—I didn't want to lose three years of training.

I tackled the problem with my usual zeal. I buckled down to the rigors of intense study, taking three and four lessons a week and vocalizing every spare moment I had. People must have wondered who this crazy gal was, walking down the street humming and doing breathing exercises. It was completely unacceptable to me that my voice might not improve or that I might not have a career in the music world.

It was becoming increasingly obvious, however, that all of this effort was not improving my voice much. Even when I did seem to be in good voice, I struggled with my allergy and would have to interrupt a song because of a choking fit.

"Why don't you give yourself and your voice a rest for a while?" Maestro finally suggested. "You are young and perhaps this thing will right itself." To me it seemed he was saying, "You don't have it any more. Why don't you just give it up?"

I did quit. The sensitive, tender side of me groped for an answer: why were one's dreams so elusive? The night of my last lesson I lay crying, wondering why my existence seemed to be such a catastrophe. The night and my sorrow threatened to devour me. Was my life ever going to work out the way I had planned it?

I had worked at the Holiday House for about a year while continuing to work for Dr. Paskan to help pay for my singing lessons, when I heard about a restaurant that needed a food and cocktail waitress.

"I have a feeling you'll be just right for this place," said Mr. Ricardi, the owner of the Horn Restaurant. "I'd like you to start Thursday night. I hope you like spaghetti, that's our main dish here. You'll be eating lots of it!"

Not only did I eat lots of spaghetti, I cooked and served plenty. When the Ricardis were not there in the early evening, the job of cooking the steaks and spaghetti fell to me. I faked my way through at first. One night a large group came in for dinner and I was alone. As I rinsed the cooked spaghetti in a colander over the sink, it got too heavy for me and I dumped it all in the soapy dishwater. The steaks were done. I didn't have time to cook more. I fished the spaghetti out of the water, doused it with *lots* of sauce and confidently served it. Every bite was devoured and my secret was not known.

Some very well known people frequented the Horn and sang there just for the pure pleasure of it. I would get an opportunity to sing once in a while, and it was great. My past dream and failure haunted me at times, but I learned to deny the hurt and just soaked it all in, living vicariously through other people's talent.

"Hi, love, how's our favorite girl tonight?" Mr. Fowler and his wife came in three or four times a week. I was fond of them both, and besides, he always left me a generous tip. They both drank too much, and at times I would overhear them arguing over the fact that he gambled.

"Rudy, you say that to me every time, but you go right back and do the same thing all over again. You're driving me to drink!" It was like an echo from my past. I felt sorry for them and wished they wouldn't fight.

Mr. Fowler mentioned his son Rodger and what a great guy he was. "I don't like that Pat he's dating. She's pretty, but she doesn't have a brain in her head. I'd like to see Rodge with a gal like you. How about it?" Rudy asked.

"Well, I don't know. Why don't you bring him in one evening?"

"He's been wanting to see what's so great about this place," Rudy replied. "I'll ask him why he doesn't come and see for himself."

I saw him the minute he walked through the

door—walking tall with relaxed shoulders, a smile showing his beautiful, even, white teeth. His mouth crinkled at the corners and his soft, wavy-brown hair was combed back neatly as if to control the unruly waves. He looked confident and yet shy. I immediately noticed the soft cashmere of his bottle-green jacket. He and the blonde with him sat at the piano bar.

"Good evening," was all I could get out.

"You must be Joni," he responded. "I'm Rodger, Rudy and Billy Fowler's son, and this is Pat." Pat was a bit cold and unfriendly. We talked about the restaurant and his parents but I wasn't paying too much attention to the conversation. I was captured by his warm, sensitive blue eyes, which, without being aggressive, caught mine and drew me gently to him. He was remarkably handsome and his body was lithe and lean. I felt a bit flustered and hoped I was saying the right things.

A few nights later Rodger came in again—alone. It was quite late. He ordered a glass of beer and lingered over it until closing time. "I'm not much for keeping these late hours, but I'd try to stay awake if you'd go out for a bite to eat with me." We went to a nearby coffee shop that stayed open all night. I was too nervous to eat. My heart was pounding. I sat and drank tea while we laughed and talked. I didn't much like talking about myself, so I listened as he told me a bit about his life. His parents had been divorced when he was two or three years old and his mom began to drink. She met and married Rudy when Rodger was five. Rudy was good to Rodger and there was a great deal of love between them, but Rodger was quite unhappy that Rudy and his mom both drank—too much. Rudy's gambling was quite a concern to Rodger also.

I heard in Rodger's soft-spoken voice the hurt of a heart burdened with the disappointment of a confused and unhappy family life. Their big smiles and boisterous laughter were masks they all wore to hide the sadness inside—masks like the one I wore. I stared into his eyes, falling in love with a kindred soul.

The next few weeks we somehow managed to spend a lot of time together. Rodger was studying art and working at 20th Century-Fox Studios. I, of course, was working days and nights, so we spent Saturday and Sunday together. Some week nights, after having a nap, Rodger would come in and wait for me to get off work. We would go somewhere and just talk and talk. We very guardedly shared some of our dreams with each other.

The months flew by and I was happier than I had ever been. True love had come to me at last. Rodger was my knight in shining armor, come to rescue me. Life was about to begin. I couldn't wait for the time when Rodger and I would plan a home and fully share our life together. Everything he did told me he was getting ready to ask me to marry him, and I knew what I would say.

One night we had driven to Malibu for dinner at my brother's. After a warm evening together, we both were feeling relaxed from the two drinks we had shared over Larry's thick, stuffed pork chops. I thought of how at ease I felt with Rodger, and how much I loved him. As we left, I wondered how long I could conceal the depths of my feelings. He must know how I feel, and yet, do I risk putting it into words? We stopped to watch huge, luminescent green waves wash upon the shore. Could he possibly know the same powerful surge was going on in me, washing over me and bathing me in its warm glow? He was especially tender. He drew me to himself and held me for a long time. My heart pounded and I heard myself saying, "Rodger, Rodger, I love you so."

"Joni, I've loved you from the beginning. You're all I need or want. I think a June wedding would be perfect, don't you?"

And of course I did.

3

"Those whom God has joined together let no man put asunder."

I stood in the little chapel looking out at the surrounding silver-blue lake, and watched the gentle June breeze playing in the willowy trees. I heard the lazy buzz of a bee somewhere in the room. Shortly before, I had walked down the aisle holding my father's arm and briefly felt his pride and love for me that day. The warmth of my love for Rodger was welling up within me as I listened to the pastor's words. This was a forever kind of love. How was I, who had always felt so unloveable, fortunate enough to have a love like this? "O God, please don't let it be a dream," I whispered inwardly.

After a short honeymoon in Monterey and Carmel, we settled into our new apartment and began to live out our dreams. I couldn't have been happier. I wondered why mom and dad had such a difficult time together. Rodger was always warm and tender, and we had such lovely fun—when we could be together.

I was still working my two jobs, and we had to scrounge for time. The weekend days and my two evenings off became precious to me, especially Saturday nights, when Rodger would come into the restaurant about midnight, have a drink while he waited for me to get off, and then take me out to breakfast.

My conception of the love and intimacy of married life included hours of sharing hopes and dreams, and solving fears and problems. Time became increasingly important to me as I hungered to get to know myself and my husband better, and achieve something beautiful together in our marriage.

But Rodger tired easily and felt that being up late wasn't good for him. "I've tried taking naps so I could be awake when you get home from work, Joni, but the interruption of my sleep pattern just leaves me shot the next day. I need to rest more. I'd appreciate it if you'd be quiet when you come home." I stared at him in disbelief.

"After only a few months of marriage you don't want me to disturb you when I get home?" I asked incredulously. I felt frustrated enough to start a battle, but Rodger was quietly adamant and that was that. Besides, I was sure he didn't mean every night. But this was wishful thinking. Night after night, I would lie staring up at the ceiling, longing to talk to the heavily breathing figure beside me, to be taken into his arms and loved.

"This is not the way it's supposed to be," I thought. "I've got to do something." In my mind, Rodger was withholding his love from me like my parents used to. So I fell into the same role I had with them, and tried to earn his love and approval. I had loved buying little gifts for

24

Rodger anyway, but now every week was like Christmas. The nights we ate at home I prepared all of his favorite dishes, and we dined by candlelight. Although I was not much for watching TV, I endured all of his favorite programs. Rodger had a little black Thunderbird that he loved to work on, keep polished and go for drives in on Sunday afternoons. I helped him with the car and made sure I was always along on the drives. Yet there was a distance between us and the gap widened. Because neither of us knew enough about ourselves, our discussions of our innermost feelings were halting, often trailing off inconclusively, abandoned as we hit a brick wall.

Why is he so afraid of closeness? I wondered. Does he know how terribly lonely I am? Why am I so afraid to tell him? I buried the hurt. I seemed to have lips of clay and the words never came out, except in real anger.

One night as I was leaving for work he said, "Joni, I'm going to be working on some drawings tonight and I'll wait up for you. Maybe I'll have some scrambled eggs ready. How does that sound?"

"Just great! I'll be home as soon as I can." That evening I could hardly think of anything else and I sang all the way home, looking forward to a delightful, intimate time with my husband. But I walked into complete stillness, a single low light illuminating a note placed on the TV set: "Joni, I had to wax the car tonight as well as do some tough work on the drawings. Just had to get some sleep. I'm so tired."

My whole body flushed with helpless rage. What good would it do to wake him up? I had found that Rodger avoided all confrontations, and would usually keep his peace and then make a fool out of me with my own words. I got angrier just thinking about it. Then I recalled his car—the recipient of his energies that evening instead of me—parked out front, across the street from a new construction site. I ran outside to the freshly broken ground and picked up huge clods of dirt. With all my might I flung them at Rodger's shiny black idol, sobbing and throwing until I had no more strength to lift another ounce of dirt. As I walked past the car on my way back to the apartment, I noticed the paint was chipped and the hood dented. I didn't care.

Rodger was a very early riser, and I usually got up just in time to get him a quick breakfast. But this morning, spent from the emotion of the night before, I lay in bed until he left. I held my breath as he walked outside. A few moments later he walked back in, looked at me and quietly said, "What the hell, Joni?" He grabbed some things out of his drawer and softly, in measured tones, he said, "I'll be staying with my mother." Without a backward glance he was out the door.

I had wanted some response from him, some effort at communication. But this passive stance—! I hated him.

A few days later we patched things up, and Rodger came home. Things were better for a few weeks, but we were soon back in the old pattern and I began to put tremendous pressure on him to show me that he still loved me. He didn't seem to notice. I longed to hear him say he loved me—and I wanted to say it to him, too, but seldom did. I was afraid I wouldn't get any response.

The glow of Christmas and the warmth we had shared with family and friends were still clinging to me. I was feeling a real sense of closeness with Rodger and was unusually affectionate. I decided to risk being the loving wife I wanted to be, and Rodger responded—soon it was time to leave for work.

"Joni, I wish you didn't have to work tonight! I'd just like to hold you here in my arms the rest of the evening—it's been so special."

"Please set the alarm for midnight and come on down to work. I don't want to end this night leaving that place alone. Besides, I'm so proud of you when you come in—I love it when I can show you off! And this can be continued later," I laughed.

"Okay, sweet one, I'll see you then. This has been so much like a honeymoon, maybe I'll carry you over the threshold when we get back tonight!"

Midnight came and went. Then 1:00. Now it was 2:00 and time to close. I had thought about calling home, but I didn't want to seem too eager, so I let it go. When I got home about 2:30 there he was, all tucked in, snug and warm on this cold December night, sleeping like a baby. There was a pitcher of water left on the dinner table. I went into the dining room, picked up the pitcher, calmly walked back into the bedroom, and dumped the whole thing on Rodger's head.

"Thanks for the great evening!" I hollered. "You might as well be dead for all the living you do!" I knew I'd never win his love back this way and yet I couldn't help myself. I felt driven to vindicate my bruised feelings, to lash out at the disappointment that threatened to rob me of the only thing I valued in my life: Rodger's love. I rushed out of the room, flopped on the couch crying, and hoped he would come and apologize. If he would, I would. I knew I had been wrong, but something in me had been crushed, and in trying to sort it all out, I blamed Rodger for how I was feeling. Darned if I'll be the one to say I'm sorry, I thought. Feelings of rejection seemed to threaten me. I couldn't understand why Rodger acted as though he didn't love me any more. He had once loved me, and I was still the same person. Just then he waltzed by with the now familiar announcement, "You can reach me at my mother's place."

It was two weeks later that on my way home from the Horn, I felt an ominous feeling in my stomach and pulled the car over. I was violently ill at the curb. From then on, it seemed I was in a constant state of nausea. I went to the doctor, who listened to my symptoms, ran a routine test, and confirmed what I had suspected: I was seven weeks pregnant.

I knew my face reflected my joy when I got home. Rodger looked puzzled by my expression.

"What did the doctor say?" he asked.

"We're going to have a baby!" I blurted out excitedly.

"Oh, no," he said worriedly.

"What do you mean?"

"I'm simply not ready to be a father. I want you to think about an abortion."

"Not even for a minute!" I retorted, aghast.

"Well, you'd better," he said, walking to the bedroom where he began throwing some things into his suitcase, "if you ever want me to live with you again."

Soon he was gone, leaving me alone with his dreadful words. Well, not quite alone: I put my hand on my abdomen. I had another person to think about now. Perhaps he just needed more time to let the idea sink in a bit.

When I went to see him in the hopes of a speedy

reconciliation, I found he was absolutely adamant about not having the baby.

"I will not be a father and accept that kind of responsibility at this time in my life. Besides, I don't think we can make a go of our marriage. I still want you to consider having an abortion. And I'm not coming home." I became hysterical.

"How can you be like this, how can you do this to me—to us? I love you and I want to have your baby more than I want anything in the world!"

"I think you had better calm down and leave," Rodger said. Leave? My heart was breaking and I wanted him to take me into his arms, tell me he loved me and that everything was going to work out all right. I wanted him to be as excited as I was over the child I thought we had conceived in love.

Rodger's brother came in and told us both to calm down, suggesting we talk later in the day. Rodger said, "I've said all I have to say." I left, feeling drained and hopeless.

A strong March wind was blowing with heavy rain that had been falling all of this dark and dreary Sunday. A blue and white Ford convertible was careening down Sunset Boulevard. The car turned up a dead-end street heading toward the little church at its end. There was road repair going on, and the mud from that and from the hill above, mixed with the heavy rain runoff, was pouring down the sides of the street.

Suddenly the car began to spin. It seemed to take off in all directions, and then it smashed into a nearby telephone pole. The convertible top split from front to back. The door flew open and my unconscious body spilled out face down into the rushing mud. Then all was silent.

A doctor living on the street wondered if the terrible sound he had heard had been the wind blowing that wavering pine tree in his front yard over onto a car. He rushed out; his heart quickened at the sickening scene that met his eyes. He yelled to his wife to call an ambulance and the police. Then he lifted my lifeless form from the mud and began clearing out my nose and throat. I had nearly drowned in that muck. As he covered me with the blanket his wife had brought, he noticed one shoeless foot grotesquely twisted, obviously severely injured.

"What's happened? Where am I? Why can't I move my leg?" A nurse came over.

"You've been in an accident—five days ago. You're in the hospital with a broken ankle, and you've got a cast on up to your hip."

"Oh, no!" I cried out, and began to weep. I was soon to learn she hadn't told me all. "What about the baby?"

"Baby? The baby's okay." Then I heard my dad's voice.

"How you doin', kid?" He took my hand, and there were tears streaming down his face. Where was my mother? I knew she cared, and I always thought dad didn't. What a strange paradox. Where was Rodger? Oh, boy. A jolt of pain shot through my body, and then I remembered.

I had driven to Dr. Paskan's office when I left Rodger. I had a key to the medication closet, and committed a terrible breach of trust, feeling ashamed and yet not caring. I counted out thirty Nembutal, and swallowed them all. I later found out that my stomach had been pumped as standard practice for one brought in unconscious. That routine procedure saved my life.

Thirty Nembutal and still alive—a miracle. Oh, I had desperately wanted to die. I had felt such pain in my heart, such terrifying aloneness. Alive again, and now this broken body. What a ghastly surprise.

There was a flurry of activity as new IVs were started in my arms, which were all black and blue. The month before I'd been in this very hospital with both arms—and sometimes hands and feet—full of needles. I'd been having a rough pregnancy and difficulty keeping anything down. I had tried to continue working, finally becoming so dehydrated I collapsed and spent three days hospitalized.

Good grief! Where was Rodger, then and now? Didn't he care about what I was going through to have his baby? I was at a dead end. No one had anything to offer. Why couldn't I just die? I wept, "Dear God, help me." I said it over and over, but it didn't seem to help. Sleep was the only way to escape this nightmare.

"Be sure that x-ray apron covers her abdomen—I don't want this girl touched without all the proper precautions being taken." My obstetrician saw my alarm as I woke up, and went on to explain that when I was first brought in after the accident, a lot of x-rays had been taken without any precautions to protect the baby. No one at the hospital had known I was pregnant. If the baby was all right, it would be a miracle.

I was drawing breath with stabbing pains. They were x-raying my chest to see if anything was wrong. After what seemed like a very long time, a nurse came in with a doctor I'd not seen before.

"Young lady, I don't like being the bearer of more bad news, but you have a collapsed lung. I'm going to have to make an incision into your chest and insert a tube to inflate your lung." Right there in my bed after a local anesthetic, he cut into my chest and inserted the tubing.

"Oh, Lord!" I cried, as the searing, red hot pain seemed to go on and on.

"That's a mild statement for what I've just done—think I'd be inclined to cuss a little if I were in your shoes." Finishing up, he said, "We can probably get you out of this contraption in three or four days. Hang in there!" I looked at him.

"Do I have a choice?" He laughed, and shook his head.

"You've got a comedienne in there," he observed to a nurse. But I wasn't laughing. Each time I drew a breath, the inflating lung would touch the tube and send shock waves through my system. I would writhe until I'd be so far down toward the foot of the bed that the nurses had to lift my cast and me back up toward the head. I was given injections for the pain, but because I was allergic to most of the drugs, the doses had to be minimal. The days and nights turned into one long, black hell, and I begged to die.

I drifted in and out of consciousness for several days. On the fifth day, they removed the dreadful tubing and sutured up the little incision in my chest. At last I could sleep.

I awakened about dawn. There was my father. What was he doing here at 5:00 o'clock, I wondered. As I stirred, he came over to my side.

"I couldn't sleep and decided to bring some of my paperwork down here. You seem better this morning. I'm so glad." His eyes were misting.

Soon the silver rays of the early morning sun drifted into

the room, and I remembered that this was Easter Sunday. The sunrise was beautiful, the pain was subsiding, dad cared—and I was going to have a baby, Rodger's baby. I was looking forward to motherhood. I was reminded of new life, the Resurrection. Maybe there *was* hope.

Later that day, mom, dad and Larry came by to visit. I was more alert now than I had been, and I became aware they seemed a little uncomfortable. They tried to appear relaxed, but their faces betrayed their nervousness. I thought, my parents are afraid and hurt—hurt because their daughter is lying nearly helpless and in essence it was by her own hand. They didn't say it, but I felt that was what they were thinking.

My mom was standing near the door and I heard her exclaim, "Oh, here comes Rodger with an Easter lily." I hadn't seen him but once since I'd been in the hospital, and my heart quickened as he entered the room. I was warmed by the sight of him. He gently touched my hand.

"Hi, Joni."

"Oh, Rodger, it's good to see you—sorry I'm such a mess and made such a mess of everything—" my tears were choking off the "I love you" I had wanted to speak. Rodger didn't have much to say. He stayed away from my bed and seemed rather cold. Before long he left and I sensed something was wrong. As I began to cry softly, my mother came over, picked up my hand and told me what my fears had already told me.

"Rodger isn't coming back, Joan; he told us the other night."

The doctors had told him there was presently some doubt as to the outcome of my foot injury and when I would be able to walk again.

"He told the doctor and us," mom continued, "that he simply could not handle the responsibility of a crippled wife and baby. He said, 'Anyway, our marriage just hasn't been that good lately, we'll be better off without each other.' " Mom started crying then. "That dirty b------! When he told your dad and me that, I pounded my fists on his chest and told him what a rotten coward I thought he was."

My mind was a whirl of thoughts. What am I going to do? What if I can never walk again? Who will take care of my baby? I wonder what it's like to have a baby and no husband. Does he have someone else? What a scene that must have been between mom and Rodger. Rodger is over six feet tall and mom is so short and frail. He just stood there and let her hit him—out of guilt?

"What's going on here? Why all the tears?" Dr. McGonigle was a jolly, outgoing man, obviously filled with the "milk of human kindness." He turned to me. "Where's that smile of yours? You know you cheer us all up." After getting a weak smile out of me, he looked thoughtful, and cleared his throat.

"Wednesday morning I am going to have to do some surgery on that ankle."

"Why?" I asked. "I thought you had set the fracture when you put this big cast on my leg."

"Well, that was a temporary measure; we've been waiting for you to get a little stronger to complete the diagnosis. There were so many other minor things wrong, and we wanted to find them all and get them out of the way first." Then for the first time since the accident I learned just how my ankle had been broken. "Apparently upon the impact of your car with the telephone pole, you were thrown out of the car, but somehow your high-heeled shoe caught under the brake and your foot was caught there too, causing your ankle to be literally torn in the grasp the brake had on your foot. Now we're going to do our best to repair the damage." He explained the procedure, but the only part I heard was, "Then we'll put a pin in your ankle and see how it goes from there."

"Will I be able to walk again?" I murmured.

"We have every hope," he replied. "Ask me again in a few weeks." There it was again! The fear, the panic, the utter despair.

Oh, God, why, why? I just want to die—why didn't you let me die?

During my weeks in the hospital, a love and a warmth I had not known began to bloom between my mother and me. Mom liked being needed, and I certainly needed her now. I was looking forward to living with them upon my discharge to complete my recovery and my pregnancy. Mom and dad were excitedly anticipating their first grandchild.

It was a luscious spring day when I left the hospital, and though I was outside only for the few feet between the hospital and the waiting ambulance, fresh air and singing birds lifted my spirits, and I was optimistic about the future.

I was still quite weak and as yet unable to try walking with crutches, so I had to stay in my parents' second-floor apartment for a few weeks. I was glad to be out of the hospital, but I felt like a prisoner of my weakened body and large cast.

Mom and I were together constantly and she began to

just pour herself into my life. I felt the same love for her I had felt as a child, when I wanted so much for her to love me back. This time I knew she did. She really cared, and it felt good.

I hated being so useless though. I had worked hard all my life, making my contributions and holding my own. As soon as I was strong enough to walk on crutches, I learned to lean on them and free my hands to do ironing, dishes and whatever else I could to help my mother.

My foot was not healing well. The baby was getting most of the calcium in my body. Just about the time I thought I was due to have the cast cut down, Dr. McGonigle, x-rays in hand, announced, "The fractured bones in your ankle are just like an egg shell—I'm afraid you'll be keeping this hip-high cast for some time to come."

"Oh, no," I replied, "with summer coming on, how can you do this to me?"

"Just get yourself a coat hanger and carefully scratch down inside your cast when the itching gets too bad," he laughed. Boy, did I use a lot of coat hangers that summer! Because of the seriousness of the injury, I was never allowed to have a walking cast, so my crutches and I became good friends during those long months of recovery.

I spent a lot of time wondering what was going to happen to me and what I would do when I finally left my parents' home. After all, I couldn't expect them to take care of me forever. Deep down I clung to the hope that Rodger would come back and be the man I needed. I still loved him very much. I knew in a way I always would. I was so sure he'd come back that every time the phone rang, my heart would skip a beat waiting to hear my mom say, "Just a minute, Rodger, she's right here." I ignored the fact that he hadn't cared enough to check on my condition since the day he walked out of my hospital room.

My heart would say, "He'll come back, and when he does, I'll forgive him everything." My head would say, "Who needs that rat? I can do without him." And I said to God, "Please send him back."

My due date was September 15, and I had hoped the baby would come that day, because it was Rodger's birthday. However, at exactly midnight on September 13, just after I'd said good night to mom and dad, I lay down in the bed in what seemed like lots of warm water! I immediately began to have contractions.

"Mom, mom, this is it," I yelled. "My water broke and I'm a mess." Dad came rushing in.

"Keep calm, kid. Everything is going to be okay," he said nervously. My mother called Dr. Meitus who told her to get me over to St. John's Hospital in Santa Monica right away. Mom stacked towels around me and dad reassured me, "Don't worry about the car. If it gets wet it'll clean up again." Upon our arrival at the hospital dad announced, "Girl, you're not going to try and walk up those stairs with crutches in your condition. I'm going to carry you." But for a reason I didn't understand, I didn't want my father to carry me. So with my usual independent flair I said, "No, I want to make it on my own."

"Don't be so darn stubborn. I *am* going to carry you. You'll never make it otherwise."

I was determined to do it my way, however, and began the difficult journey up the stairs. I was quite a sight and the moment we got to the admissions desk the clerk grabbed me and plunked me down in a wheelchair.

"Delivering a baby in your condition is going to be quite a feat," one of the nurses quipped.

"I'm used to doing things the hard way," I laughed.

After eight hours of hard labor, I was about to deliver the baby. Because of my lung problem, the doctor gave me a spinal block rather than total anesthesia. I was delighted to be awake because I wanted to see my precious baby the minute it was born.

"Just one more deep breath," Dr. Meitus encouraged. "I think this is about it."

Through clenched teeth I joked a bit with him. "If it's a boy, you can put him back."

He was still laughing when he said, "You'll have to keep it; it's a girl. By God, it's a girl!" A few minutes later I was told I had a healthy eight-pounder with lots of curly hair and blue eyes.

"Oh, hallelujah," I sighed.

As I was wheeled out of the delivery room, Larry rushed over to me and hugged me. We both cried together for what seemed like a long time. Out of the corner of my eye I could see Dr. Meitus and my mom with their arms around each other, dancing in the hall, saying, "It's a girl, it's a girl." I heard him exclaim, "By golly, after all she's been through, she deserved to have her girl." I couldn't have agreed more.

After seeing that sweet little baby, knowing she too was alive and well, I was beside myself with joy. I drifted off into a peaceful sleep. Later that day when they brought her to me and laid her in my arms, I knew there was a God and then and there I dedicated Lisa Michelle to Him. I said, "Father, she is yours. Please help me to be a good mother.''

The four days I lay in the hospital, I was positive God would send Rodger back to me. Now that the baby had arrived, how could he resist? I envisioned him bounding into the room with an armful of flowers, taking us both up into his arms, and declaring all the wonderful things he was going to do for us. Every day and every night, I listened to the footsteps in the hallway, and held my breath whenever they approached my doorway. "Please, God, let it be him.'' But it never was.

Joyful and excited to be a mother, and loving my baby girl, I was still sad and terribly lonely. Rodger had never shared the joys of pregnancy with me—the anticipation, seeing and feeling the baby move, the plans and dreams that approaching parenthood brings about, or the thrill of the actual birth. Now he was never to share in raising his daughter, never to know the joys and heartaches of being a parent for the first time.

Frequently during my convalescence, new hope would flame up in my heart that God was going to work everything out.

When Lisa was a few weeks old, my final cast was removed, and out came this skinny, misshapen, scarred, hairy leg!

"Is this really me?'' I gasped. "Will I always look like this?''

"Well, a good shave will help for starters,'' chortled Dr. McGonigle.

I looked at him with big tears in my eyes.

"Would it be all right to see if it still works?''

"You're going to be stiff and sore for a few weeks, but

you can begin to bear a little weight on that ankle now. However, don't throw away the crutches just yet, you may feel the need of them for a week or two."

A couple of weeks later I concluded my foot wasn't just stiff, my heel would not touch the floor. After an extensive examination Dr. McGonigle explained, "Your Achilles tendon has atrophied somewhat from being in the cast for so long. Some exercise may help, but it might never be totally normal. You're still a walking miracle though, young lady, and if you wear the right height heel and practice on your gait a bit, no one will ever know you came so close to being crippled."

A few weeks after that I experienced another miracle.

"Well, Joni," Dr. McGonigle was settling back into his chair after his usual examination, "your body's been doing its work. That ankle's looking better all the time. In a way I'm sad to say it, but you're not going to have to come in quite so frequently for checkups any more. In a few more months I'll probably have to discharge you."

"You know, doctor, that makes me think of something I've worried about for several months now. I want you to know that I'll be getting a job soon. And when I do, I'll start paying you everything I owe you for all your wonderful help."

"Just a minute, Joni. Just a minute," Dr. McGonigle interrupted. "You have a baby and a future to think about now. That's enough. Don't worry about the past. You don't owe me a thing. I'm just happy to see you well and strong again."

"You mean—" the tears were uncontrollable. "Why?" I finally managed to sputter.

"I already told you, Joni. Just accept my gift and go find

yourself a job and raise your baby.'' A tiny tear glistened
in Dr. McGonigle's eye.

"Sure, I'd love to have you back. You can work as
many hours as you think you can handle right now,'' Dr.
Paskan said.

"Dr. Paskan, it means a great deal to me to have your
forgiveness for taking the medications from your office.
How can I thank you?''

"Don't try to earn it, Joni. It'll be good just to have you
back. See you Monday morning.''

I went back to work, increasing my hours as the weeks
went by. And each afternoon I rushed home from work to
see Lisa. How I loved her! She was all mine and I would
take good care of her. I loved bathing and dressing her.
Each evening we took long walks as I proudly pushed her
down the street in her pretty little carriage. I loved to hear
my dad when he came home in the evenings: "How's my
baby doll? How about letting gramps hold you for a
while.'' Then he would fuss over her until she was smiled
out and nearly asleep.

Time flew, and after the first of the year, I knew it was
time to think about leaving.

"Mom, I found a darling apartment in Brentwood and I
can move in on the first of the month.'' Neither of us said a
word about why I had chosen Brentwood, but we both
knew. Rodger lived only a few blocks from there.

On moving day, mom started digging in the back of a
closet for some of my clothes that had been stored for
several months. I heard her groan.

"Joni, you'll never believe this—what are you going to
do?'' I rushed into the bedroom to see the clothing she had

tossed out on the bed, riddled to shreds by moths! But I was too exhilarated about moving to get upset.

"It's a good thing I mostly wear uniforms. I'd get picked up for indecent exposure if I wore any of those!"

Dad and my Uncle Bob both pressed a little money into my hand as I left with my last load. We had gotten my furnishings out of storage and so, with fewer clothes, lots of baby paraphernalia and high hopes, Lisa and I entered a new chapter in our lives.

One night shortly after we had moved the telephone rang.

"Joni, this is Rodger. I'd like to come over and see the baby. Would you let me in if I came by?"

Could it be true? My heart pounded and my mind raced. But out of my mouth came only bitterness.

"What kept you?" This was what I had wanted so badly, and yet my anger popped right to the surface. I could have kicked myself. He came the next evening.

"She's beautiful, just like her mother," he said, as he sat holding Lisa and looking at her as though he could not believe she was real. My heart melted like April snow. Lisa took to him and they both seemed to enjoy themselves.

"I'd like to come back and see you both, if you can stand my face after all that's happened," Rodger said.

"That's fine with me." I wondered if I dared to allow myself to feel what I was feeling. I not only wanted him back, I did not want him to leave ever again. Only a few weeks earlier I had filed for divorce on grounds of desertion, and here I was, letting him kiss my cheek, saying, "I'll call you tomorrow."

We began to date, and he spent quite a bit of time at the apartment with Lisa. He enjoyed being with her, and at first, he and I enjoyed one another's company. But before too long, some of the old problems surfaced. Even though we talked of getting back together, we could not get our relationship on good enough footing to make a permanent arrangement out of it again.

After a few months he called less and less, and his visits became infrequent. The writing was on the wall, and I accepted the decline of our relationship without too much of a struggle this time.

"What beautiful curly hair you have," I said, trying to put little Annie at ease. She had an upper respiratory infection and her father had brought her to Dr. Paskan for treatment. She was obviously frightened, and as I took her pulse she cried a little.

"Do you think I'll have to have a shot? I'm not really that sick, am I?" Her pretty blue eyes implored me. I fell for her instantly. We chatted a bit and then Dr. Paskan came in to examine Annie. Yes, she did have to have an injection.

"But I'll be real gentle," I assured her. Afterward, I hugged her, and felt her little arms tight around my neck. Her father, Bill, noticed this too.

"She's having a difficult time. Her mommy went to heaven a few months ago."

A few days later Bill was back with Annie for a final checkup. She put her arms around me again, not in fear this time, but in greeting.

"You're pretty," she told me. I picked her up.

"Not as pretty as you are, Annie."

"Daddy, let's take Joni to lunch with us." I glanced interestedly at him. He was beaming from ear to ear.

"Pumpkin, I've always told you what a smart one you are." He looked at me. "Do you think you can put up with us for an hour?"

"Sure, if you can wait forty minutes for my lunch break."

"You betcha. See you in the waiting room."

Over lunch I learned more about the two of them and they learned that I did not live alone.

"I love babies," Annie said. "When may I see your baby, Joni?"

"Soon," I promised.

Bill told me his parents took care of Annie most of the time, and a neighbor who had been close to his wife took her the rest of the time.

"We've got a nice little home in Culver City. Just right for us. And Annie's fast becoming the lady of the house."

"I liked it better when mommy was with us," Annie countered.

Bill told me she had died of cancer after a few months' illness. I didn't need anyone to explain the sadness in Annie's eyes or the eagerness with which she approached me. I longed to take her in my arms and say, "It's okay, Annie. I'll take care of you. Everything's going to be all right."

I did a lot of thinking after that lunch. And soon I was telling my mom about the potential new man in my life.

"He's very nice looking, mom, always smiling, pretty curly blond hair, close to six feet tall, and very, very sweet! Oh, yes, he mentioned the church they go to, so he's got that in his favor, too. It seems like a good idea to date

44

him. Don't you agree?"

"Well, just take it easy. Don't open yourself up to being hurt. It sounds nice, but who knows? What does the guy do for a living?"

"I really don't know. He's in some kind of secret work for the Air Force. He said he couldn't talk about it. I just know I think he's nice and I'm looking forward to seeing more of him. I know he's going to ask me out, and I'm going to accept. Please don't worry, mom. Everything will be all right; I just know it will."

Bill did ask me for a date and, over a long, leisurely dinner, we began to share some of the details of our lives with one another. He was warm and sensitive and readily related to some of my feelings. When he walked me to the door that first evening, I knew he was as attracted to me as I was to him. Bill took my hand. His eyes were moist.

"I know it's too soon to anticipate such things, but I believe the four of us would be absolutely perfect for one another. You seem to be my dream of the ideal woman. I'd like to spend as much time with you as you can spare."
Usually I didn't like people crowding me like that, but right then it felt good. We made plans to meet at my church the next morning for Sunday services and then voted in favor of taking Lisa and Annie for a stroll in the nearby park.

We laughed and talked all that next day. The rapport I had instantly sensed between us was growing swiftly. Annie and I got better acquainted too. She was a sweet little thing, warm and sensitive like her daddy, easy to love. She was delighted with Lisa and took great delight in making her laugh and looking after her.

Over the weeks we got to know each other better and

better. Bill was masculine and bright and obviously enjoyed my womanliness. I began to feel I was regaining my balance through my relationship with him. I knew he was getting serious and I liked the idea. Our times together were always happy ones, and it was good to be free of intense problems.

After a three-month courtship we were all sitting in the park on an unusually warm day. I was kind of daydreaming, watching the sun dance off the little pond nearby. My reverie was broken by Annie's voice as she skipped over to the quilt on which we were lounging.

"Daddy, is this the day you're going to ask Joni to marry you?"

Bill's face became solemn as he momentarily looked startled, recovered, and then said, "Yes, this is the day! How about it, darling, will you marry us?"

"Oh, you two, what could be better than for the four of us to be together as a happy little family? Yes, you guys, I will marry you!"

Bill immediately added, "A happy family, yes—a little family, no. I hope we have a dozen more kids!"

I hoped he was kidding, but I didn't ask.

Two and a half months later we were married in a quiet ceremony with only our families present. I could hardly say my vows through the tears. We had walked into what I thought was a ready-made situation, and I was sure God had had His hand on it. My pretty pink dress and lovely ivory roses were crushed by all of the hugging and kissing that went on from both sides of the family. I was elated and looking forward eagerly to being a wife again.

I wondered just how honest I was being with myself, though. Right during all that hugging I was thinking back to telling Rodger of my marriage plans. I had hoped he would ask me not to. "Oh, well," I thought, "that's behind me now, and I'm looking forward to the future and a normal, happy life."

We settled into the little house in Culver City and I was content to fall into the role of homemaker and mother. Not long afterwards, Annie hugged me one night after we had said our prayers together and, looking at me with those imploring blue eyes, she said, "Joni, may I ask you something important?" She was a bit hesitant and I couldn't imagine what was coming.

"Sure," I said, "why don't I snuggle down with you and we'll just chat awhile." It took her a few moments to work up to it and then she flushed a bit.

"Could I call you mommy now?" My heart flowed over and so did the tears in my eyes. I told her how proud and happy I would be if she did.

Almost immediately after we were married I became aware of certain things I had not noticed before. Like the little innuendos with sexual connotations, the dirty jokes and the words I didn't like, words I had not heard on Bill's lips before we were married.

Where he had been considerate and gentle in our intimate life during the first weeks of our marriage, he became selfish and almost brutal. My objections were often met with a brutal "Shut up! What do you think women are for? What did you expect? You knew I had been without a woman for a long time due to Edna's illness."

"I thought you loved me."

"What does love have to do with anything?" he growled.

Soon, Bill began to show up on Friday evenings with a bottle of bourbon under his arm. At first he would just suggest we have a drink, but soon it was a demand. I would go ahead and have a couple of drinks with him, just to numb the agony of what inevitably lay ahead later in the evening. Saturday nights were a repeat of Fridays. But amazingly, on Sundays, off we would go to church, just like normal people!

"My God, what is this all about? How can you behave like this all weekend and then go to church?" I chided.

"One thing has nothing to do with the other," Bill insisted.

I knew he was wrong and I was becoming frightened because several times he had slapped me and thrown me across the bed. I wondered what had happened to that nice, quiet, normal life I thought I was headed for.

One evening Bill came home and began to tell me about a couple he knew at work. He very carefully explained to me the "fantastic outlet and enhancement of their marriage" in their wife-swapping activities. Bill bluntly told me he wanted to go to one of their parties that weekend.

"You can go but I'm staying home," I sobbed. "Don't ever even mention such a thing to me again." With that I walked out of the house, slamming the door behind me. "I hope I didn't wake the kids," I thought.

I walked down the street in the light of the full moon, oblivious to everything around me. "God, I've made another mistake. I've got to get out of this mess and soon." I wondered if God was listening. Would He even consider one tainted with such evil? I turned my wretched self around and headed for home.

Intuition told me Bill would be sweet and try to con me when I got there. Sure enough, he greeted me with open arms.

"Honey, where have you been? I was really worried about you. No matter, you're home now. We won't talk about this again until you feel like it." Well, I knew I was *never* going to "feel" like it, but I also knew that wouldn't really stop Bill.

Something else began to bother me. Annie, Bill's seven-year-old daughter, often had nightmares and would cry out in her sleep. But when I ran to comfort her, Bill generally came in to say he would stay with her awhile. Then he would sleep in little Annie's bed with her the rest of the night.

After a good many such episodes I told Bill, "Annie is going to have psychological problems later on if you continue to share the same bed with her. Anyway, she's having nightmares more often now than ever. Can't you see the unconscious manipulation going on? If she has nightmares, daddy will sleep with her instead of Joan."

"Joni, I don't need you to tell me how to raise my daughter, and I'm not interested in some theory you picked up in a book." That was the end of that. I broached the subject several times more—to no avail.

It wasn't long before I found myself really hating Bill. "What happened to that sweet, gentle man I used to know?" I wondered. I didn't understand what was happening. I was still me. What had caused Bill to turn into such a kinky monster? I decided the only hope for us was some counseling. I broached the subject with Bill.

"Honey," I sweetly said, "I don't want to fight any more. What do you think of speaking to the pastor or going to a marriage counselor?''

''No way. Most of those guys have worse problems. I'm not about to spill my personal life to one of them. Besides, the only problem we have is with you and your damned puritanical upbringing. I don't want you going either. You'll just get more confused than you already are. You've read too darn many books. Why don't you just try being a woman for a change?'' I looked at him in disbelief.

''That last remark was just too much. You don't want a woman, you want some kind of a pervert for a wife!'' I screamed. ''Well, you haven't found one in me. And I'm not going to become one just to please you.'' I stormed out of the house again, running as fast as I could. I didn't know where I was going. After a while I went home, crawled into the back seat of our car and lay there crying for a long time. I thought about Lisa and what would happen if she should awaken and need me.

All sorts of thoughts came rushing to mind and I wondered what possessed Bill to sleep in the same bed with his own daughter, and felt a fear for my own daughter rise up within me. I told myself I'd better go inside. I did, but not until I'd made a decision.

The next morning I called a mover and made an appointment for the following Monday morning. Then I called my mother. I had already told her a little bit of what had been going on.

''Mom, I can't stand it another minute, I'm getting out. I'm afraid to tell Bill. I just don't know what he would do to me.'' I explained that I was moving out on Monday while Bill was gone. She agreed to be there as soon as Annie was off to school to help me get packed.

I found an apartment and then wondered what I would

do for money. I called a friend named Lee who worked in a very busy restaurant to see if they needed any help. She said they did and suggested I go in for an interview. Soon after that I was sitting in Harry Jacobs's office. Harry was the owner of the Hi Hat restaurant.

"Joan," he said, "if you're as good as Lee and Rubin say you are, you're hired." Rubin had been a cook where I had worked before, and now he was working for Harry Jacobs. He was black, and he and his wife and I had become good friends. He had been cleaning house for me on a weekly basis since we had met. The day I brought Lisa home from the hospital, there was Rubin at the door. He was the first person outside of the family to hold her and the first one with a gift—a ten-dollar bill, which I needed more than anything at that time. How nice it would be to work with my friend Rubin again. I told Harry when I could start and it was settled. I was beginning to feel better about things.

What really bothered me was Annie. How could I not tell Bill and still tell Annie? How was she going to get along without me? "Oh, well, Bill's parents are here half the time anyway, and the rest of the time Annie spends at their house. I'm sure they'll love caring for her again," I consoled myself.

I couldn't wait for Monday to come. After Annie left for school, I placed a note on her bed that I'd written the day before. Then I called Bill's parents to say I wouldn't be home that afternoon, and could they pick Annie up from school and keep her until later that evening? Then I began furiously packing. Mom and I were nearly ready when the movers came for the few things that belonged to me, and off I went to face the world alone again.

The following week, after a scant nine months of marriage, I filed for a divorce. But my sense of failure did not prepare me for what happened soon after in my parents' lives. After thirty years of marriage, my mother called one day and very calmly said, "How would you like to go apartment hunting with me today?"

"For whom?" I asked.

"For me!" Mom had threatened many times to leave, but over the years I'd gotten to the point where I never paid any attention. "I've had it with Dean, and this time I mean it. Please come over and get me, I want to do it now before I change my mind."

"Good grief, mom, I can't believe this is happening!"

"Well, it is, and nothing is going to stop me."

Mom moved out and filed for divorce. It was an adjustment she was never to fully make, and I wonder now if the breakup of their home had a direct impact on the strange choice I was to make in the not-too-distant future.

4

Dave walked into the Hi Hat one evening, as he did every evening, and said, "Joni, it isn't good that a young and beautiful gal like you never has any male companionship." I looked at him suspiciously.

"That'll be some time in coming, Dave. I'm really not ready for much of a relationship with anyone right now."

"Be that as it may, I have a business associate I'd like you to meet. I'm going to bring him in one of these nights. From there, who knows?"

"Dave, I can't stop you from bringing anyone in here, but don't play Cupid. I'm simply not interested. I need time to recover from some of the things I've been through. And I have a degree of contentment now, so why rock the boat?"

The following week, Dave walked in early with a tall, older man.

"Keith, I'd like you to meet my friend Joni." We chatted a moment, and my only thought was that he seemed like much more of a gentleman than the people I generally associated Dave with. Dave jovially announced, "The drinks are on me." In between a couple of drinks and shoptalk, the men had light conversation with me. They were paying the bill and about to leave when Keith turned to me.

"Joni, I like you; I like you a lot. What are you doing in a place like this?"

"Maybe I'll tell you someday," I responded.

A couple of evenings later Keith came in again. He had just left his office and I liked the beautiful beige vested suit he was wearing—it set off his sandy hair. To me, he spelled real class. As we chatted, I was charmed by his directness and his unaffected attitude. I was a little put off that most of the time he stuttered quite badly. It embarrassed me. I had never known anyone who stuttered, and I didn't know what to say when the conversation got difficult.

After two drinks, Keith said he'd better be getting home. "Told my son I'd do the cooking tonight." I wondered about this but I didn't comment. "I just want to tell you one thing before I leave. Joni, I'm going to marry you."

"That bourbon does give some people a loose tongue," I laughed uncomfortably.

Keith began coming in at least twice a week, always complaining, "I don't like this place. I wish I didn't have to come in here to see you. When are you going to say you'll go out with me?"

"Never," I answered. "You're too pushy to suit me. I have a feeling you're used to getting your own way, and, right now, I just need some room to breathe. Besides," I

54

got bolder, "I don't think I like you." By this time we had gotten around to talking about our personal lives, and I had come to admire Keith. But still I found him abrasive and cold, and that put me off.

Keith had been divorced for ten years, and he and Jane were still friends. But he seemed quite bitter over what the divorce had cost him financially and in terms of his standing in the community. He was from a place in Ohio that he called "snob hill," and some of snob hill's snobbery had rubbed off on Keith. He was very proud of his background and instilled a bit of this in his son, Jason. Jason was sixteen. Shortly after Keith's divorce, it was discovered that Jane had tuberculosis and had to be treated in a convalescent hospital. So Jason lived with Keith.

Keith was a manufacturing representative and loved his work. I marveled that with his stammering problem he would choose sales as a career. Because he owned his own agency, he was always trying to get new lines, and he traveled and entertained frequently. He asked if I would hostess a hospitality suite the following month during a convention in Los Angeles.

"You'd be perfect. Everyone would be drawn to your warmth and charm. I don't have a secretary right now, and even if I hire one before then, she couldn't do the job you could. How about it?"

"Well, I don't know. What do I have to do?"

"Just mingle with the guests. Chat and be yourself. I'll even buy you a beautiful gown for the part. Now you can't turn that down, can you?" I was pensively considering it when he added, "Come on, sweetie, I'll pay you and pay for your baby-sitter too."

"I'll think about it."

"You know, Ace—I'm going to call you Ace because you're number one in my life—you are exactly what I've been waiting for these past ten years."

My head was swimming as I went to bed that night. The setup was a natural. Lisa certainly still needed a father, and Jason still needed a mother's influence, even at age sixteen. I was tired of working until two in the morning. And Lisa had begun screaming for me to stay home.

There are two problems, I thought. First of all, even though I admire and respect Keith, I'm not in love with him. And isn't this the same situation that not too long ago I also saw as ready-made? Will the pieces of the puzzle fit together any better this time? I fell into a troubled sleep, and dreamed a dream that had recurred for years. I was in a room with no doors or windows, banging on the walls in terror, screaming for someone to let me out. I awoke to Lisa's sweet voice humming in her bedroom, and I felt comforted. "God, please help me now," I murmured.

I was glad, as it turned out, that I had accepted Keith's invitation to hostess his business party. I had always thought of myself as a rather shy person, and yet I didn't feel shy at all. That night I chatted with the wives, kidded with the men, and saw to it that there was plenty to eat and drink. Keith was proud of me and beamed all evening.

"This is the girl I am going to marry," he announced to several of his close associates. They spoke their approval and I pondered what to do. Keith was eighteen years older than I, and I wondered what his guests thought about that. I had often wondered what Jason thought about it. I was thirty, closer to his age than Keith's.

On the way home, Keith stopped the car. "I've got to talk to you now, Joni. I don't like not being able to see you when I want to. With my working days and you nights, it doesn't leave much time for us to be together. I want you to quit your job.''

"Quit my job?" I gasped. "I've got to make a living. I can't quit my job!''

"Yes, you can. I'll subsidize your income until we decide what we're going to do about our relationship. In the meantime, you can help me a bit in the office, and come along when I entertain my business guests. You'd be a great asset to me, just like you were tonight.''

"Good Lord, I can't take money for doing that—and I'm not about to let anyone support me! What kind of person do you think I am?" I was quite offended and Keith knew it.

"Okay, I have a better idea. We're both gun-shy about marriage, and yet, I can't get along without you, and you need me too. So let's go down to Mexico, tell our families we're getting married there, and come home and set up housekeeping as 'husband and wife.' How about it?" I was mortified.

"I can't believe you'd ask me to do such a thing! What happened to all this talk of marrying me?''

"Well, you've turned me down any number of times now, and this seems like the perfect answer. I'll be good to you and it wouldn't be any different if we were married. No one need know. And I think we'd both try harder, knowing the other could just walk out at any moment. I love you, Ace, and I won't be satisfied until I have you for my own.''

"No wonder you're top in sales. You never learned to take no for an answer." We were both quiet as Keith drove on. All at once I blurted out, "I don't know if I love you or not!''

"I don't care. That will change after we've lived together for a while. You'll have a lifetime to learn to love me.''

After Keith dropped me off at my apartment, I turned on the stereo and found myself dancing around the room. To be wanted, to be needed, to have security and a home and a father for Lisa—what more could I want? It's a risky business for the future, but I've had that little piece of paper before, and someone to say all the right words, and look where it got me. I caught myself wondering if it really was a sin. I had always been among those who felt that the snide remarks about common-law marriage held some truth. Funny, now I didn't feel quite the same. And within a few weeks I had consented to the plan.

As we began to talk about the "honeymoon" we would have in Mexico, I became more and more excited. Once Keith and I were together, I could stay home with Lisa, and take on the challenge of being a mother to a sixteen-year-old. Keith was so proud of me he took delight in showing me off to his friends. The prospect was rosy.

But my conscience kept nagging at me. I knew I would be ashamed if anyone ever found out. Keith and I discussed this at great length, and he finally agreed to find someone to marry us.

"It won't be legal,'' he said, "but if it makes you feel better, it's all right with me.''

Mom moved into Keith's house for the ten days we were to be gone to look after Lisa and Jason. Keith and I flew off, telling everyone we were going to marry in Mexico so his father, who lived there, could be present. We did visit Keith's father, but told him we were going to be married in

Cuernavaca, in the garden of a beautiful resort.

In Cuernavaca we started looking for the city official Keith had been told could marry us, Mexican-style. After spending hours driving through the maze of colorful, narrow streets, we found the address and Keith told me to wait in the car. Shortly he came back.

"He isn't here and won't be for several days. Waiting for him would spoil our whole itinerary. Let's just find a local church, say our vows to one another, and consider it done. Okay?"

I wanted to cry as we sat in the ancient little Catholic church, holding hands, watching ragged old men and women straggle in to light candles.

"I love you, Joni, and I take you for my wife, to have and to hold, to love and to cherish, all of my life." This seemed romantic on one hand, and a sham on the other. I really didn't know what to say. With tears streaming down my face, I looked up at Keith.

"I hope this lasts forever. I'll try to be a good wife. Thank you for loving me."

"Mommy, you came back! I didn't think I'd ever see you again." Lisa stood there with as pitiful a look on her face as I had ever seen.

"Of course I came back, darling! Didn't you know I would? I missed you terribly and I love you very much. I'm so glad to be home with you. Now come inside and tell me what you've been doing while we were gone."

We had called home twice and knew already that Lisa had had hives, a bad enough case to have been treated by a doctor. He felt she was upset over the "marriage" and my being gone. I didn't see it then, but Lisa was horribly jealous of Keith.

A few nights after arriving home, Keith and I were having tea after dinner, and were engaged in an engrossing conversation. Lisa and Jason had just come in from romping on the front lawn.

Lisa said to Keith, "Why don't you get out of here? I want to talk to my mommy." Jason was the first to answer as only a sixteen-year-old could.

"Aw, Lisa, what's the matter with you? You can't talk like that. Why don't you just act your age and shut up?" Then he tried teasing her out of being angry. It didn't work, not in the long run.

Jason and Lisa liked each other and both adjusted quickly to being brother and sister. I was touched by their obvious affection for one another, and the companionship Jason offered Lisa. It was Jason who first suggested a move.

"This part of Westwood has too many old people in it. Take our street, for instance. There isn't a kid near Lisa's age within six blocks of here. I think we should move. I'd like a swimming pool anyway. After all, how can you live in Southern California and not have a swimming pool? What do you think, dad?"

"Well, I've been thinking we need a bigger home—"

A few days later Keith brought a realtor home with him. "How about it, Joni, want to spend some time with Charlie here scouting out houses?"

"Oh, fun! I'd love it! It'll be a brand-new experience for me."

The fun soon wore off as we traipsed through house after house searching for the one we all liked or that Keith thought was a good buy. We were about to give up when

Charlie suggested we look at a house in the hills above the San Fernando Valley.

"The Valley!" we both exclaimed. "Who wants to live in the Valley?"

"It's a great house," Charlie said, "and the people are about to leave town—they're getting desperate and I think you can get a good deal."

"Okay," I said, "but it's absolutely the very last house I want to see."

The next morning, as we walked into the heavily ferned and flowered yard, I exclaimed, "Oh, this is beautiful!" I had a great sense of excitement as we stepped inside. I stood at the sliding glass door of the family room, looking out on the huge pool, imagining Lisa and Jason cavorting there. I had never seen such a large kitchen and the island range caught my eye. The valley floor spread out beyond until the mountains rose up to enclose the sweeping view.

"It's a dream house! Oh, Charlie, this is my house, but do you think Keith will buy it?"

"He's crazy if he doesn't," Charlie replied.

Sure enough, he loved it too. We moved in during some of the hottest weather of the year, and the kids practically lived in the swimming pool. I soon found I loved gardening, digging in the warm earth and inhaling the fragrance of the roses and other flowers I was planting. I had a deepening tan, and felt physically and mentally fit and strong.

I easily submerged myself in my new life style of full-time wife, mother and homemaker. The new kitchen was fun, and although I had always been a good cook, I was improving my skills and impressing Keith's many business guests with my culinary productions.

Entertaining consumed a lot of my time. I loved the process of selecting the furnishings and decor to put together a beautiful home.

We were all content and life seemed better than it had in a long time. But somehow, I couldn't completely escape the undercurrent of guilt running through me all the time. I tried to throw it off, but it came back every Sunday while I sat in church. I was a hypocrite, living with Keith in a common-law marriage.

"What do you think the neighbors and your high-and-mighty friends would think if they knew we weren't married?" I asked Keith one night when I was especially irritated. We had had too much company that week to suit me, and I was sick of hearing Keith inevitably refer to me as his "young and beautiful *wife.*"

"I'm not your wife and I don't feel like one right now. I feel more like a hired hostess."

"Joni, keep your voice down, the kids might hear you and that would be a disaster. As far as the friends and neighbors are concerned, it's none of their business. Anyway, they aren't going to find out." He looked at me wearily. "I don't know why you're always bringing this up of late. I feel married to you. You're the perfect wife. So what's the problem? Maybe it's just that some of your puritanical ideas are getting in the way." Keith often chided me about being a Puritan and when he did, I felt flattered and insulted at the same time. I kept trying to deal with my conflicting feelings. I couldn't understand Keith's motives at times.

He had a habit of observing to anyone we'd meet, "Isn't my wife a handsome woman?"

"Keith, I hate that word 'handsome.' It seems

masculine to me. But no matter what you call me, I resent being shown off. I'm like a thing instead of a person. Please don't do it any more."

"Ace, you know how proud I am of you, I just have to say something. I'll continue to admire you in front of my associates, and I'll do it my way. You may as well give up and accept that fact," he laughed.

"Keith, this isn't a joke! Please listen to what I'm saying."

"Joni, you can't change me. I'm too old and set in my ways. Just learn to mellow out and take things as they come. Aren't you glad I admire you so?"

"No, I'm not. I have the worst feeling you do it mostly to control me and keep me from getting out of line." After a few moments of silence, I began to weep. "Keith, I feel more like a possession than a person. I want to be loved for who I am, not because you find me attractive and helpful in your business dealings."

"Joni, you're being ridiculous. I do love you, just as you are. It's just that you fit into my life so well. But that's only an added bonus. I would love you even if you didn't. You're being too sensitive about this. Don't you have everything you want? Haven't I been good to you? What more assurance do you need?"

"Good grief, I give up! You don't understand a thing I've said. Can't you see that I want you to take the time to know me, the real me, the things that make me tick? The outward appearance isn't even important. Why do you make so much of it?" Keith came over and put his arms around me.

"I know you're a good woman and that's all I need to know."

But I needed to know more.

I began to demand constant reassurance of Keith's love for me. He had neither the time nor the ability to assure me of my worth and his love, but I pressed him to do it more and more. There was never a saturation point. I couldn't be filled. I began to feel more and more empty and less and less like a woman.

What am I? I wondered. I just seem to be a great empty pit. Will there ever be anything to permanently fill up that space? I didn't have an answer.

When I was young, I spent most of my time trying to please my parents. I nearly killed myself trying for Rodger's love and appreciation, driven by the resentment that had built up over the years when I had felt no one loved me. I was really blinded by that anger so I married Bill, and had allowed that roller coaster ride to dump me onto Keith's doorstep. Now here I was again, trying to please Keith and all of these strangers—all for a little recognition!

"Keith, I'm sorry, but I can't get into this thing like you do. Half of these people I'll never see again. I don't care about them and they don't care about me."

"Joni, I don't understand you. I thought you had a good time doing this." I did at first; I enjoyed the attention. But like a narcotic, as I took more and more the payoff got smaller and smaller. The truth was that I had been feeling the strain so much, I had begun to wonder if I was going to lose my mind. There was still an emptiness in me that craved to be filled—an emptiness no one could reach, like a tomb that had been sealed off.

The meaninglessness of my life began seeping into my consciousness like a poison. As I grew more despondent, I ate more. Our busy social life gave me plenty of opportunities to drown my sorrows in food. And cocktail hour was always a must with Keith. My weight began to slowly creep up, until I suddenly realized I had gained twenty pounds in my five years with Keith.

"Oh, Joni, he's just a fantastic doctor and I feel great. I've already lost ten pounds. You've just got to go." My neighbor and good friend, Jean, and I had been to another weight loss doctor previously, whose regimen and medications had left me feeling the worse for it.

"Okay, I'll make an appointment to go with you on your next visit. I hope this works, because I'm beginning to hate myself."

"Hi, gals, how are y'all?" Is this teddy-bear, homespun fellow the doctor?

"Joni, meet Arnold. He's a Texan like me. Guess that's why he's so likeable. He'll have you as beautiful as ever in no time." I was not prepared for a weight doctor who was himself so chubby. After we left I voiced my misgivings to Jean.

"If he's so good, why isn't he thin? Do you really think he can help us? What about the adage, 'Physician, heal thyself'?" We both laughed. "Another thing that bothers me is that small, shabby office."

"He told me he hasn't been in Los Angeles too long, and he intends to move into nicer quarters as soon as he gets established. Anyway, what's the difference, as long as we lose weight?"

I discovered in Arnold a warm and compassionate person. In some mysterious way, he gained my confidence without my even knowing it. He seemed to really care about what I had to say. I did something completely out of character: I told Arnold about my marital situation. I told him what I had so glibly lied about to everyone else, the words "married" and "husband" tripping across my tongue in conversations.

"Joni, I think I can help you with some of your problems. I'd like you to try a few hypnosis sessions—it could do wonders for you right now. There's nothing to be afraid of. You wouldn't do anything under hypnosis that you consciously disapprove of. It's really very relaxing."

"Okay, you're the doctor. When do we start?"

"Right now. Just sit back, close your eyes, and relax. You are going into a deep sleep, deeper and deeper—" Eventually I became so conditioned that all Arnold had to do was touch my forehead and say "Sleep," and I would be under. I didn't like the thought that another person had this kind of power over me, and after several weeks, decided to discontinue the sessions.

Arnold eventually moved to larger, much nicer offices, and his practice increased. He soon needed a second girl in the office and asked me if I was interested in the job.

"Well, I've talked about going back to work recently, and Keith just has a fit. He says my place is at home and that I shouldn't talk such foolishness. Come to think of it, lately he comments on how foolish just about everything I say is. Anyway, it's been over five years since I've worked; I don't know if I'm sharp enough any more."

"There you go, girl, putting yourself down again. Where is that self-confidence we've talked so much about?" Arnold asked.

"Guess I don't have much any more." Tears started welling up in my eyes. "I just feel like an ant—a little old ant."

A couple of weeks later, when I arrived for my appointment, Arnold was in a frenzy.

"Joy just went home sick and I'm trying to do everything myself. Do you think you can stick around and help out for a while?" Lisa was visiting my father in the mountains, and Keith would be out to dinner with clients, so I said yes. "You're an angel in disguise. Now I'll just go back to doctoring and leave everything else up to you."

I called Keith to tell him what I was doing. He mumbled a weak, "That's nice, hon. See you tonight." I knew he wasn't happy—but I sure was. I fell right back into the old routine. Assisting with the patients and managing the front office seemed so natural. I loved every minute of it!

"Wow, you're something else, gal! You really get the work done. We worked together like we've been doing it for years! I don't think Joy will be well enough to work tomorrow. Could you come in the morning and help out again?"

"Sure, I can. With Lisa away, it won't be any problem."

"How about dinner, Joni? You must be starved. I sure am." We had worked to 9:30. I wondered if I should go. I had already heard through the grapevine that Arnold and his wife had been separated several times and that his marriage was on the verge of collapse.

"I'd better call home first. If Keith is there, I'll just go on home." But he wasn't. "Okay, you're on. Hope your pockets are full, I could eat a mule!" I was a little worried about what Keith would think when he found out.

Over dinner we discovered we had much in common.

Arnold told me of the grief and bitterness he still felt over the death of one of his four sons. It was scary, but I let my heart go out to him. I was being drawn again to someone who needed me. I looked into his gentle eyes and told myself I was safe with him.

I got home before Keith, and rushed to get ready for bed so he wouldn't know how late I'd been out. I decided not to mention I'd gone to dinner with Arnold. Keith got home pretty soon after that.

"How's the working girl? Have a hard day at the office?"

"Don't be nasty now," I replied. "Actually, I did work hard but it was fun. Arnold has asked me to help out for the next couple of days while Joy is out. What do you think? I'd like to."

"Would it do any good to say no? You're a free woman."

I worked with Arnold three more days, arriving early to be ready for the day's load of patients. I felt refreshed, almost exhilarated, to be working again. On my last day, Arnold called me into his office.

"Joni, this place can't run properly without someone like you around. Would you consider working three days a week? Maybe that way you could work and keep the peace at home."

"I'd like to—very much—but I think I should talk it over with Keith. Let me call you in a couple of days."

Keith was upset. "I was afraid something like this was going to happen. I don't like it. And what about Lisa?"

"I can get someone to be here in the afternoons when she gets home from school."

"And what about me? Who's going to be here when I

68

get home from work?''

"Whoever stays with Lisa can start dinner for you. I promise not to work late, and besides it's only three days a week.''

"I don't think I could stop you anyway. Go ahead and try it for a while.''

Around the office I began to see the lack of organization and made suggestions to improve its efficiency. Soon I changed the bookkeeping system to a more updated one, and talked to Arnold about the fee structure he had set up.

"You're practically giving your services away. My gosh, Dr. Paskan had a fee schedule similar to this fifteen years ago! I don't see how you can get ahead this way.''

"That's something I've been wanting to talk to you about. This is just the first of several offices I want to set up. In a few months I'll be ready to open a second one. I'm going to need an office manager and you'd be perfect for the job.'' I was astounded as he went on to offer me a percentage of the gross earnings. I was enjoying my extra cash, but this was different. It might mean big money. Was I up to it?

"I really need you. I couldn't handle this without you!''

He knew how to get me. "Well, it would be a challenge. I don't know if I could handle two offices, but I'd sure like to give it a try.''

"Great! You can start by looking for another location with me next week. It'll be a few weeks before we can do much. That'll give you time to work things out at home.''

Work things out, I thought. If only it was that easy.

"I hate the idea!'' Keith was fuming. "Darn it, Ace, you're supposed to be a homemaker, not the breadwinner!''

"It's time I tried my wings. I want to do something besides cook and clean and pull weeds all day. I've felt so lonely and bored. Keith, please.''

"Can't you find a different form of expression? Is this your way of rebelling because we haven't married?''

"Keith, I'm not rebelling; I'm just trying to find myself.''

We both knew it was settled in my mind and Keith didn't say too much more about it.

"Put'er there, pard,'' Arnold said the next day as he extended his hand to me. "We'll be the best team around. We're going to make a real name for ourselves, you'll see.''

Both offices were doing well. Lisa had adjusted to having a housekeeper, and Keith tried to hide his discontent. If Keith wasn't happy, I told myself, he was getting what he deserved for treating me so coldly over the years, not caring about the real me. I was on top of the world, a success. I felt like somebody again.

Arnold was in the middle of the grief that goes with divorce. He started working long hours, which meant we spent more time together. I felt compassion and a deep fondness for him. I found it difficult to leave the office sometimes. It was my new home.

Keith approached me one evening. "Maybe we made a mistake in not getting married,'' he said pensively. "Joni, I feel you slipping away from me. I still love you, and I don't like it. Would you quit your job if I were to marry you?''

What a question! Earlier I wouldn't have thought about it twice, but now I heard myself saying, "It's too late for that now. I don't know where our relationship is headed, but I don't think it's to the altar, not now."

When the words came out, I realized for the first time what I had not yet admitted to myself. My feelings were greater for Arnold than for Keith. A wave of guilt and apprehension swept over me. It seemed I had no control over my emotions as they ran rampant in one direction and then in another, like leaves caught in a whirlwind. In my quandary, I consulted Arnold.

"Joni, you don't love him or belong with him. It's probably much too soon," Arnold said hesitatingly, "and I may hate myself for this one day, but I want you to think about marrying me. I love you and need you." All I heard were his first few words.

"If you love me, why did you say you might hate yourself one day?" I was hurt.

"Forgive me. Please forgive me. I don't know why I said such a thing. I've known for a long time that I was in love with you and wanted to marry you. We are good for each other and I know we could make each other happy. We already seem to be filling so many needs in one another."

"You make me feel so good about myself, Arnold, so alive, so vital and real. I can take my mask off and just be me around you. I need you—but another marriage? I've been such a failure in the past. It's kind of scary. Let me think about that for a while."

"Take your time, darling. I can wait. Anyway, the way my divorce is going, it will be a long time before we could be married." He took me into his arms and hugged me close. "Joni, Joni, I adore you."

Sleep wouldn't come that night—or the next, or the

next. I was torn by the guilt that had come upon me like dark gloom. I wanted to tell Keith what I was going through and yet I was unable to get the words out.

Arnold wasn't making things any easier. Flowers and other little gifts began to appear on my desk every week—adorable cards, notes, poems. He said and did all the right things, and I was falling head over heels in love with him. Thinking this might be my last chance for real happiness, I wanted more and more to be with him.

I knew I couldn't lead a double life. I gathered all my courage and went to Keith. With tears in my eyes, I told him, point by point, why I was leaving him.

"You're making a mistake." His voice shook. "Please stay. We'll get married and I'll do all I can to make you happy. You can't just walk out like this after six years!" Keith had always been the strong man, in full control. He rarely showed his feelings, but he was crying now. We sat and hugged each other and wept together, but I was not to be persuaded.

During the next few days, he said everything he could to convince me to stay. Jason came home from Berkeley and we sat up nearly all night talking together. He, too, wanted me to stay. That was hard. But if no one was making it easy on me, I guessed I was getting all of the pain I deserved.

I felt so confused and helpless, I decided I would talk to my dad. I flew to Bakersfield where dad picked me up and drove me to the place he and my stepmother had in the mountains. We talked over all the pros and cons and he encouraged me to leave. One thing he told me was a deciding factor.

"The last time I dropped in down there, you were at work. I walked into the house to find Lisa in her room and

Keith demanding she come out. She had taken a large spool of some of Keith's wire samples from the garage and had woven a web of wire across her doorway, attaching it to heavy objects in the room.

" 'What's going on here, pumpkin head?' I asked her. She cried out, 'I don't like him and when mommy is not here I don't want to talk to him!' " Dad went on to say that he had talked to the housekeeper, who told him Lisa spent most of her time alone in her room when I was gone in the early evenings.

"Well, what do you think?" the broker asked.

"It's a fantastic house, all right—I can't believe it!"

The next day Arnold and I took Lisa to see it, and I told her then that we were moving. She didn't seem upset, only enthusiastic about the house.

"To show you the seriousness of my intentions," Arnold said, "I want to put the house in your name. You've lived on shaky ground long enough!"

I insisted on making the payments. "It'll be like paying rent—it's the least I can do."

Arnold agreed to that and added, "Don't worry about me. I work late in the evenings and spend Saturdays with my boys. And now I'll be spending Sundays with you. I don't need anything else outside of my little old apartment."

I packed up my belongings and my daughter and moved out of Keith's home the next weekend. This time I'll make it, I told myself, or die trying.

We began fixing up the house and yard, immersing ourselves in our new home. Lisa was more her old self again, much more content. She looked forward to our marriage, saying Arnold would "make a neat daddy."

Arnold and I did seem the perfect couple. We were both completely involved in his practice, which brought us even closer together. The practice was growing and we each had more money than we had ever had, and we enjoyed spending it.

Arnold decided to visit several physicians in Europe to study their methods, and to our delight, he took Lisa and me along. We stayed in the best hotels, dined in the finest restaurants, had private guides and chauffeur-driven cars. It was heady stuff for a gal from Nebraska!

After a year and a half had elapsed, we decided to set a wedding date. We went to the pastor of our church.

"I don't know you two very well. I love you both, but you're asking a hard thing." He forced the words out. "You've both been married before, and the church takes a dim view of remarriage after divorce."

My heart stood still. "You mean, we can't be married in our own church?"

His face showed how crestfallen he felt. "I know how you feel," he began, "but the Bible is pretty clear on this matter. Besides, I've been very concerned lately about the divorces right here in our midst."

I was no longer listening. Through hot tears I said, "If we can't be forgiven right here in our own church, then where are we supposed to go? We'll get married anyway. Do you want us to go to the courthouse and have a judge perform the ceremony? Don't you suppose God has forgiven us? Why can't you?"

"Joni, it's not a question of forgiveness. I don't judge you and I have nothing to forgive. Let me pray about this awhile. In the meantime, I'd like to see the two of you several more times—just to see where you are in this relationship and perhaps counsel you both a bit. Okay?"

We left the church in a pouring January rain. It was cold, but no colder than my heart. Now the church was rejecting me. The old guilt, always just beneath the surface, began to rise up within me. A sense of foreboding came over me. Perhaps this was a sign we were not to get married.

Arnold and I kept our appointments with the pastor. The question of our marriage did not come up again. Then one day the pastor called.

"Joni, do you guys still want to get married?"

"Of course! Have you made a decision?"

"Yes, I have. I'll perform the ceremony gladly."

"We'll set a date and be in touch with you soon," I said matter-of-factly. As I hung up, I wondered at my lack of joy. I called Arnold and told him the news.

"Great! Let's set the date soon, darling—I'm ready."

Then it struck me! Was I ready? I wasn't sure.

Over the previous months I had begun to see Arnold as less than the perfect man I had thought he was. I recognized an immaturity in him that bothered me. Could I trust him? Would he let me down in a crisis? I talked to mom about it.

"If Arnold doesn't do some growing up, you're going to have your hands full. Sure, Joni, he's a sweet and thoughtful guy—but it's going to take more than that to make this marriage work. I hope you two can handle it."

"Mom, I don't know what to do. Part of me loves Arnold, and part of me doesn't. Sometimes I think I hate him, he makes me so mad. I have a lot of doubts and fears about the future, and I feel almost remorseful for having gone this far. But how can I back out now? We have this house. Lisa is excited about having Arnold as her daddy.

I've left Keith and I'm up to my ears in the practice. I'm in too deep to back out now."

"Joni, I wish I could help you, but I don't have any answers—I can't seem to help myself."

"This is crazy," I said, shaking my head in a daze. "I really don't want to get married, and yet I feel trapped."

The day of our wedding arrived. We had a beautiful, very touching ceremony. Arnold held my hands and gazed into my eyes, his love shining through like a flame. His look, the pastor's words, and the sense of the closeness to God I often had in church softened my heart and I was ashamed of my doubts. It was just a short time ago that I had been convinced I loved Arnold more than I had loved anyone—since Rodger.

God, help us to make it, I silently prayed.

But as the soloist sang, I remembered the dream I'd had the night before. I was walking down the aisle with candles so huge I could hardly carry them. Just before arriving at the front of the church, I fell on my face before everyone. They laughed, my mother's laughter rising above all the others. What could it mean, I thought, and felt again a sense of foreboding.

The pastor signaled us to kneel at the altar. As I looked up into his handsome, smiling face, I thought, Oh, God, I hope I don't make him sorry for having married us.

Arnold repeated his vows with a shaky voice and tears in his eyes. I thought how foolish I was to be feeling as I did. Wouldn't anyone feel lucky to be marrying such a guy? Why didn't I?

The organ pealed out at last and we turned to walk back up the aisle. It was time to tuck all my feelings deep inside of myself. But in photos taken that day, the best I managed was a half-hearted smile. Had I compromised again?

5

It was the stuff dreams are made of. Arnold became more well known in his field and was invited to speak at seminars all over the United States. The practice flourished as never before. I suppose we had more material possessions, more cocktail parties, did more traveling, saw more horse shows and lived higher than any other family we knew.

"Arnold," I said one evening as we were window-shopping after a movie, "I'm afraid to even comment on anything I see for fear tomorrow you'll buy it for me!"

He just laughed, "I'd try to buy the moon for you if I knew you wanted it."

We visited physicians in Romania, Switzerland and Italy with the idea of improving our skills for our practice. We became excellent business partners and worked quite well together. We worked hard and played hard, taking trips to Hawaii, Mexico, our national parks, and a couple of pleasure cruises. We always stayed in the finest hotels and ate in the best restaurants.

What was wrong?

Often, as we were planning a trip, I would think of it as the great escape. I couldn't overcome the gnawing emptiness I felt inside. Perhaps new surroundings and the excitement of traveling would help. But every place we went was just a reminder that I didn't belong.

I was constantly aware of God's creation. Standing in a meadow, looking at a waterfall, viewing the breath-taking mountains of Scandinavia, or walking through some of the world's famous gardens, I would think, God, your handiwork is incomparable; thank you for sharing it with me. In such fleeting moments I would think I had caught ahold of something lasting—but then it was gone! And I would realize I could change my environment all I wanted, but I was still the same person inside.

Arnold and I had cast ourselves in roles we were not comfortable with, and we were still two lonely people living side by side.

"Arnold," I asked one day, "why don't you talk to me any more? Why can't we share our deep thoughts and feelings with one another?"

"I don't know what you mean." It was becoming his standard reply.

"Yes, you do!" I started to boil. "You're just afraid it might cost you something to open up, be transparent, let me see you as you are. And you don't want to see me as I am. You don't even care. You're more concerned with your patients than you are with me!" There it was. I saw it clearly for the first time. I was jealous of his patients. Now it was out. "You think nothing of listening to some woman tell you her troubles for an hour, keeping all the others waiting, while you listen, chat and offer sage advice. Why don't you have time like that for me?"

He shrugged. "You're being foolish."

"Arnold, you've got to stop working so late," I persisted. "I don't want all of the money in the world. I want my husband and Lisa wants her dad. Why can't we have a normal home life? You're going to kill yourself working these hours."

"Joni, I've done this for years. I don't know any other way. When there are people to be seen, I need to see them."

"It's not as though you were a surgeon or a general practitioner. You're in an elective-type practice and those people you see at night could wait another day. I feel like your patients are more important to you than Lisa and I."

"Honey, that just isn't true. Anyway, you know how much I hate to argue. Let's drop it."

Lisa felt the disappointment too. Many evenings in the first months of our marriage she would say, "Mommy, when is Doc coming home? I want to see him before I go to bed. Do you think he'll be home in time to play a game with me?"

"I really don't know, honey. I'm sure he'll try." Sometimes she would ask me so many times in one evening that I would feel frustrated to the point of tears. She never tried to conceal her anger at Arnold. When he would occasionally arrive home while she was still up, she became cross and unresponsive toward him. This in turn made him angry.

"What do you mean telling me Lisa asks for me all the time? When I get home, she acts as though she wishes I weren't here." None of us quite understood what was happening.

He began to buy her more and more things. One day, when Lisa was only eleven, she looked at me solemnly. "I wish Doc wouldn't bring me so many things. All I want is a little more of his time." Lisa's discontent inflamed my own. I felt much more justified venting my wrath against Arnold on her behalf rather than on my own.

Arnold quickly got the message. He responded in the only way he knew how, by self-pity. He stayed away more and more, often not arriving home until eleven o'clock at night. His patients, many of them women, actually adored him. That was so much better than coming home to two angry women. Slowly I began to see at least that much.

"No wonder you don't want to come home. After playing God all day, it's hard to step down and be a regular person in your own home."

This would infuriate Arnold. "Where did you get that stupid notion?" he demanded. One night he spoke more frankly. "I don't like coming into this vacuum. How can you be so darn sweet sometimes and so bitchy other times?"

"Nuts!" I was more sad than angry. I had wondered the same thing myself, many times. We oscillated between fighting and having some really happy, loving times together. We both wanted desperately to love and be loved. We tried hard to make it happen, and sometimes, it seemed we had succeeded. But never for long.

"Honey, I want to adopt Lisa and I think it's time we talked to our attorney about it."

"That would be wonderful," I agreed. One evening

soon after, we sat down with Lisa.

"Sweetie, I don't want to be your daddy just in name. I want to adopt you and have you for my very own daughter. Your name will be changed and so will your birth certificate. You'll be a real Harper. How about that?"

Lisa looked immediately at me, and when she saw my big smile of encouragement, she looked intently back at Arnold. She did not smile. "Sure," she said. When the social worker came to question Lisa about her feelings, she responded positively enough that approval was given for her adoption.

During the proceedings, Lisa was somber, which I attributed to the courtroom setting. Afterwards our attorney said, "This calls for a real celebration. Let's all go to lunch; my wife and I are treating!" All through lunch, Lisa was quiet, and a little sad, I thought. When finally we were alone, I questioned her about this.

"I don't want to be a Harper. I'm a Fowler and nothing can change that! Doc doesn't love me. He never comes home at night and I don't feel like we're really a family."

"Lisa, why didn't you tell me this in the beginning? You didn't have to be adopted by Arnold."

"I was afraid I would hurt someone's feelings. You both seemed so happy about it."

"My God, I can't believe we went through with this when you really didn't want to." I tried to assure her of Arnold's love for her, but she sat looking at me through big watery blue eyes, adamantly shaking her head from side to side.

I had forgotten to close the doors of my mind, and my own feelings of being unloved as a child came sharply into focus. I realized that even now I felt pretty much the same way.

After the adoption, Arnold asked Lisa to call him dad instead of Doc. She listened carefully, but steadfastly refused. Arnold was obviously hurt, but he tried to hide it for a long time.

Arnold's mouth was generously curved, beautiful in laughter with its white, even teeth. And he laughed a great deal. But this morning there was no joy in him.

"Why?" He lifted his darkened face and the look in his brilliant eyes stabbed like a knife. "I can't stand the pain and humiliation of it all," he cried. "I know how hard this is on you, Joni, but I'll make it up to you someday. I promise you that!"

Shortly before we were married we had gotten into an investment that turned into a nightmare a few months afterwards. The other investors skipped town, leaving Arnold holding signed personal guarantees for which he was responsible. We spent much time in court and many thousands of dollars trying to settle our debts. During that time, one of the plaintiffs seized our bank accounts, had our safety deposit boxes sealed off and put "keepers" in our offices to take all of the money paid by patients. We had nothing to work with and Arnold borrowed money from my father to meet the payroll for a few weeks. Later we found a bank that would take the risk of loaning us a large sum of money. All of this was a tremendous blow to Arnold.

"I tried to warn you about this stupid thing in the first place. I hope you've learned a lesson." I instantly regretted my words. Why did I lash out like this? I hurt for Arnold, and still, I was angry with him. Why did I have so little control over my feelings? At other times they would be so over-controlled, that no one knew what I was feeling. Who am I, I wondered.

For several years my mother had had difficulty handling the independence she had so fiercely fought for. She had begun psychiatric treatment, during which she was put on tranquilizers. She frequently took more than what was prescribed. Mom and I fed on one another's problems until one day something happened that blew the vicious circle apart.

A lump was discovered in her breast. She underwent a mastectomy, and though she recovered physically, she was devastated emotionally.

"I'm only half a woman now. This is the last thing I need. I'll never find anyone who would want me now."

We tried to encourage mom. She spent a lot of time at our place. We urged her to get a job. But she refused. To our minds, she was choosing instead to sit and be miserable.

She took prescribed medication for pain and sleep after her surgery. To that she added drugstore tranquilizers to soothe her anxieties. Soon she became dependent on her drugs. We learned later that she was making the rounds of all the local doctors, getting them to give her prescriptions for various sedatives and tranquilizers. Eventually it became apparent she was taking too much, and Arnold and I had some long talks with her about discontinuing the pills.

"You don't understand what I'm going through," she said. "Don't talk to me about it until you've walked in my shoes."

After she had been involved in several auto accidents and had gotten to the point where her speech was slurred and her eyes glassy all the time, we became firm with her.

"Gen, you have got to seek professional help," Arnold finally said. "We want you to see a psychiatrist and go to the hospital for withdrawal." His words were gentle.

"We don't know of any other way," I whispered, my eyes on the floor, anticipating my mother's reaction.

"No!" she cried. "I've been to those shrinks on and off for years. And I've put myself into psychiatric hospitals before. I hate those places and I won't go again—ever!"

"You've got to," Arnold continued, "for your sake and everyone else's. You could kill yourself or an innocent bystander, driving in this condition. You're going to ruin your health, and you have Joni worried to death about you. If that isn't enough, what about Lisa? What kind of a grandmother can you be, doped up all the time?"

Mom stood woodenly shaking her head. She began to cry.

"I'll go for Lisa's sake, but for no other reason. I'm going to hate it, but I'll give it one more try."

We took her to the hospital a few days later. She was furious. She stayed under intensive care with a reputable psychiatrist for a month. Arnold paid all of the bills without a single complaint. Unbeknownst to us, a friend was bringing her drugs in the hospital, and she hardly slowed her intake the entire month. It had been utterly futile.

After that, she got pretty nasty towards me. One day she quite matter-of-factly said, "Why should you—and not I—have this nice home, a husband, and all the money and things anyone could want? It isn't fair."

"Mother," I murmured incredulously, "do you mean to say you're jealous of me, your own daughter? I would think you'd be happy that I have nice things, and that I am finally settled down and married again—married to someone who's so willing to do for you too!"

From that time on, I saw less and less of mom. She seemed to avoid me and I was to some extent relieved. There didn't seem to be any right way to treat her. Everything I did or said was wrong. Even when she took our monthly check and the gifts we bought, she always challenged our motives. I was confused and hurt.

Late one afternoon after I had arrived home from the office, the phone rang. Mother's therapist was on the other end.

"Mrs. Harper, I'd like to talk to you about your mother. She has a lot of resentment toward you, and I think we should talk about it in a joint session. Your mother wants this, and I wonder how you feel about it."

"I suppose so," I sighed. "I don't understand why she feels like she does about me, and frankly, I resent having to take the time for this at this point in my life. I love my mother, isn't that enough?"

"Apparently for her, it isn't. Will you come then, next Thursday?"

"Yes," I replied vaguely. Mom was being impossible and I felt angry. Nevertheless, I wanted to help, so I kept the appointment.

"She doesn't understand me!" mom was screaming. "When I say I feel ugly, she tries to tell me what a good-looking woman I am. Why won't she just let me be ugly?" She was nearly hysterical. "Why does she always think she is right? Why can't I simply be me?" She pressed her hands compulsively against her chest.

Her vehemence startled me. The doctor commented about the way she had often put her hands on her chest, and suggested she was jealous of me because I had both breasts and she didn't. Mom was irate and I was embarrassed. Finally the painful session was over.

When we left the office, mom was not speaking to me. It was several days after Valentine's Day, and I had a gift in the car for her. As we stepped into the elevator, I said, "Mom, I have a gift in the car for you. Will you come out into the parking lot so I can give it to you?" She nodded silently. She stood there looking so forlorn and frail, my heart began to melt. I wanted to reach over and put my arms around her and tell her how much I loved her, and yet I wouldn't do it. I was to regret it bitterly.

"I hear the phone ringing." Arnold rushed to open the front door. It was late at night and we were just getting home from a seminar in Las Vegas. Lisa had gone to stay with my dad for the weekend.

I was never comfortable in Las Vegas. It was too noisy, too crowded and too phony to suit me. And it was nerve-racking to be there with Arnold. He didn't ordinarily gamble, but in Vegas he would show off by throwing hundred-dollar bills around the blackjack tables.

On this particular weekend I had had a horribly uneasy feeling. Something was wrong. Several times I started to pick up the phone to call my mom. But each time I chickened out, afraid of being rejected.

I walked through the door just in time to hear Arnold say, "When did it happen?"

"When did what happen?" My heart was pounding.

"Who's on the phone?"

"It's your Aunt Faith, Joni."

I grabbed the phone out of his hands, and heard my aunt saying, "Your mom took an overdose."

"Is she dead?" I cried.

"Yes, honey, she is. She's out of her misery now."

"No! No! No!" I screamed, dropping the phone and falling to the floor where I lay screaming and crying in a curled mass on the floor. I was unable to grasp what I had just heard. Suddenly I got up and bolted out the door, running down the driveway in hysteria, screaming for my mother. Arnold brought me back into the house. Still screaming and crying, I called our pastor, but he was out of town. The pain in my heart was unbearable. Without knowing why, I called my mother's psychiatrist and sobbed out the facts.

"Why couldn't you have stopped her?" I demanded. "Was it my fault?" Then I broke into uncontrollable sobbing.

Joe, a friend of my mother's, had found her that evening. After seeing her car out front and not being able to roust her, he had called the manager of the apartment to let him in. We tried to call Joe and my brother but neither was at home.

"I'm going to the mortuary and then go looking for them," Arnold said. He called Della, a friend who worked for us, and my old friend and neighbor, Avanelle. As soon as they got there he was on his way. My anguish was unbearable and my thoughts were running wild. What good can Arnold do now? Why is he running off to the dead when he has a live wife who desperately needs him?

I was tormented by guilt for my refusal to embrace mom

in the elevator. If I had, maybe— I blurted out to Della and Avanelle, "Do you know we didn't even say good-by to one another? Mom took the little box and walked away. That was all. Now I can never say good-by."

Avanelle prayed, "Lord, forgive Joni's mother and allow Joni to forgive herself—we know you have already forgiven her."

I took little comfort. I had felt lonely many times before, but the aloneness I felt now seemed vast and unending. My friends left, thinking I was asleep, and I brooded for a long time: why? why? why?

About 5:00 on the cold, foggy February morning, Arnold returned. He sat down on the bed. "Joni, the police gave me your mother's note. Do you want to read it?"

"Will it answer the millions of questions I have? Will it make me understand what drove her to this point?"

"I don't know," he murmured helplessly as he handed me the note.

. . . All of you have been very kind, loving and good to me. Each of you in his own way has tried to understand me, but no one except God above is capable of this. I have tried, God alone knows how much, to bear pain, to reach some kind of mental and emotional balance. But all of this eludes me. Now added to this is my brother's suicide [my uncle had taken his own life one month earlier] which has crushed me. My struggle to survive and maintain my sanity has become unbearable and life is just too painful any more. God bless all of you. I love you, each one, dearly.

Planning the funeral was painful, and I didn't know where I got the strength to do the things that needed to be done. I moved about like a zombie, hardly remembering from one moment to the next what I had just said or done.

The night before the funeral, I went to the mortuary and stood looking down at mother. My mind drifted back to a Christmas Eve while I was living with Keith. My mother had made an attempt on her life. In the emergency room, I had stood looking down at her unconscious, but still breathing, form. Her blonde hair had lain loosely across the pillow. Strange, she had looked so peaceful, exactly as I'd seen her dozens of times in my life when she was asleep. I had leaned over the rail of her bed to whisper, "Mom, I love you." She hadn't heard, of course; she was too deep in her sleep. A nurse had come and stood by the bed. "We've done what we could," to which I replied, "I understand."

But now, standing in front of the coffin, I didn't understand anything. I leaned over, "Mom, I love you."

The morning of the funeral arrived cloudy and cold. On the back balcony of our home I prayed, "God, give me the strength to get through this day, and take away some of the pain."

"Joni," Arnold called, "the car is here."

On the way to the cemetery, I thought about some of the good times I had had with mom, and how much I had loved her in spite of everything, and in the face of the tremendous problems toward the end. Mom had sinned by taking her own life, and I knew God doesn't regard any sin lightly. But in his eulogy the pastor talked of how God is first of all loving and forgiving. He said God would honor the commitment my mother had made to Him.

After the service I was the last one to leave. I was holding mother's hand, wondering where her spirit was now. My pastor put his hand on my shoulder.

"Joan, it's time to leave. Your mother isn't here. I believe she is with the Lord."

"I want to believe that," I said.

"I believe that when your mother arrived on the other side, the Lord asked, 'Genevieve, do you love me?' She said, 'Yes,' and God took her in His loving arms and forgave her." I took comfort then—my mother was at rest.

But the memory of her last months was to linger on. My mother had died certain that her body was riddled with tumors. But when the legally required autopsy was done to determine the cause of death, her body was found to be free of cancer.

The closing terror of her life was soon to echo in mine. What she had dreaded most had not come upon her. It had come upon me. The pathology that had gripped my heart and mind for forty years had now taken root in my tissues.

6

There it was. My obsession had become a reality. I was terror-stricken, frozen with fear and panic, as I felt my world collapsing around me. I'm going to die, *really* die. I cringed at the thought of the pain that was imminent as the surgery loomed horrifyingly near, and then wondered if the cancer had progressed. Will there be even more cutting away at my body?

I was sure I would never be the same. I'd be Joan on the inside (maybe), but never the same on the outside. And yet I knew the disease had to be eradicated. How does the loss of one's breasts compare with the loss of one's life? I wondered too about the quality of my life from this point on. Would I be living half a life in half a body?

I thought wildly of Arnold. In one blurred image, I saw us moving toward each other in an embrace that was never completed. How would I seem to him? How would I feel to him? Would he be repulsed by what was no longer there?

Arnold, my husband, my husband. Surely I could trust

him. He would look beyond the change in me and see the unchanging me. He would know I was the woman he married. He would still love me. I had to believe that. It was my only defense against the terror that had its tenacious grip upon me.

Dr. Marks's intent gaze hardly wavered from my face when Arnold came in and shut the door.

"You've told her." Arnold put his arms around me. "Honey, I'm sorry."

"You knew all along, didn't you?" I said, referring to the delay in telling me the findings.

Dick answered for him. "Yes, we knew, but this cancer is at a stage in which it is usually *never* detectable. We had to be sure." He drew a breath. "You have intra-ductal cancer. It travels through the milk ducts, and even though it only showed up in one side on the mammogram, it's not possible that both breasts aren't affected."

"How can this be happening?" I cried. "It can't be."

"I know this is crushing beyond belief," Dick said, "but you've got to believe you're a very lucky girl. This kind of cancer seldom produces symptoms until it's too late. We've caught yours in time. I can't be sure of that until after the surgery, but that's the consensus right now."

My mind whirled as he continued. "We'll be doing a modified radical mastectomy on one side and a simple mastectomy on the other side. I'll leave you looking as good as possible."

I was not comforted.

Arnold interrupted my agony. "Honey, don't worry. We'll lick this thing together." I looked up at him. His face was drawn and tired. The only other time I had seen him look so wrung out was the day he found out we were nearly broke. For a brief moment I wondered how he was going to handle all this. "I love you and you're going to live. That's all that matters." I was grateful for his loving arms right then, but I couldn't utter a word.

I began to think about mom. I wished now I had been more sympathetic when she learned she had to have a mastectomy. I was ashamed of my callousness.

Dick broke the silence. "I want you to go into the hospital right now. We'll perform surgery in the morning."

"In the morning?" I gasped. "I can't! I've got things to do, arrangements to make for Lisa—and I need time to explain this to her."

What I didn't say was that I needed a few days to get myself together. And I had something else in the back of my mind. "I'll go in Thursday night. I want to go to a healing service at a church with my aunt Thursday morning."

Dick had been holding my hand, and tried to remain calm but couldn't. "Joni, there is not one minute to wait—we don't know if this cancer has metastasized yet or not. Every day counts!"

Arnold joined in and they both insisted that I go immediately. However, my mind was made up. Then a remarkable thing happened. The fear was still with me, but I had a numb sense of peace, and a positive sense of direction. I knew I had to go to that meeting before I entered the hospital.

I calmly explained, "It's my body and my life. I absolutely will not go to the hospital before Thursday evening."

Surgery was scheduled for Friday morning, April 21, 1972.

Sometime in the sixties, Aunt Faith had started attending Kathryn Kuhlman's monthly meetings in Los Angeles, eventually joining the choir. I began to hear about miraculous healings. One Sunday afternoon, I went to see for myself. Miss Kuhlman's manner and the intensity of the meeting made me uneasy. Yet in spite of that, I felt on the verge of tears as I sat there, somehow closer to God. But after the meeting I expressed only my skepticism to Aunt Faith, and she didn't say much to me about miracles after that until Christmas Day, 1970. She had been our guest that day and was just preparing to leave.

"I want to sit down and talk to you one day soon, Joanne," using my proper name as she always had. "God is doing some extraordinary things and I've found myself right in the middle of some of them. It's so thrilling. I want to tell you more about it—as soon as you think you're ready to listen."

I was intrigued. She had passed a few hints earlier in the day. Now she had me pretty interested. I knew one thing: she was attending a church with the odd name of Melodyland. It sounded more like a night club than a church.

"Okay, Aunt Faith, I'll let you know when I'm ready."

If Aunt Faith was attending Melodyland, I could be pretty sure it had some things in common with those Kathryn Kuhlman meetings. I didn't think I wanted to get involved in more of that. I felt a lot safer in my own church. But Aunt Faith did talk more as time went on—and I listened. She told me about their miracle services on

Thursday mornings. That fascinated me. It sounded presumptuous to actually schedule a meeting for miracles!

Now it was 1972. I was facing major surgery. My life was in danger and in two days both of my breasts would be gone. The idea of a miracle sounded more than intriguing.

That evening I phoned Jean and asked her if she would drive me to Melodyland on Thursday morning, since I didn't want to make the drive by myself. We decided to meet early and have breakfast on the way to avoid the morning traffic. It was a beautiful spring day when I stepped outside, a mantle of dew glimmering on the grass and flowers. The view from our home was breath-taking; I had never noticed before just how beautiful. Would I ever see another spring?

As I drove to meet Jean, I wondered what the service would be like. I knew I wanted to be prayed for, but I was scared. I had never gone forward in a public meeting for prayer. My mind darted back to that Kathryn Kuhlman service—people falling on the floor, others joyously praising God, still others weeping uncontrollably. I determined I would never make such a fool out of myself.

We met Aunt Faith in front of the church's bookstore. I stepped inside to buy a couple of books to take to the hospital with me. Aunt Faith said, "Oh, there's Amy, the store's owner." She introduced us, and told Amy I was having surgery the next day for cancer. "She has come all the way out here to be prayed for first," Faith said.

Right there, in front of the customers in the store, Amy laid her hands upon mine and started to pray. I was startled. No one had ever prayed for me before, especially not in a crowded room. I was embarrassed at first, but a peace and an assurance began to come over me as we entered the building for the service.

As the service began, people were raising their hands and praising God aloud. It was beautiful, and I wished I could raise my hands—but they wouldn't budge, and I couldn't audibly speak to God right then.

When people began going forward to be prayed for, I went too. I did not have the faith to believe I could be healed of the cancer, but I knew it was important to go. I asked my aunt to go with me.

A pastor came over to me and I told him I was to have surgery the following morning. He laid his hands on my forehead and began to pray. In a matter of moments I found myself in a heap on the floor. What happened next is difficult to describe. I drifted off into a deep quiet, and I felt a warmth come over me, and I was enfolded by—love. It was a kind of love I had never in my forty years experienced. I began to speak. My aunt bent down to listen. Over and over I was saying, "He loves me, He loves me, He loves me."

Never before had I even thought about whether God loved me. The question had never entered my mind. But now I could not stop the realization from bubbling up through my being. He loves me—

As Jean and I headed home, all I wanted to talk about was how wonderful it felt to know God loved me. A strange calm had come over me. It was the composure my aunt had prayed for. As Arnold, my dad, and my stepmother, Lenora, walked into the hospital that evening, I wondered how many women walked in under the same circumstances and felt as I did. Fear still lurked in the far corners of my mind, but I was distinctly calm. The fear was under control—but it was not my control.

Awaiting me in my room were flowers from the deacons of my church. Shortly a couple from church came in and prayed with me. I said to them, "This is all so strange. I feel like a spectator, that this is not really happening to me. Maybe I'm in shock," I laughed. But I knew better. I had learned what powers the mind has to dismiss and suppress the unacceptable, and something more powerful than that was happening to me. It was the love and peace of God.

Arnold was agitated, but sweetly expressed his loving concern. He hugged me. "We're going to lick this thing together." We didn't say it aloud, but both of us thought perhaps I would die soon.

I did not sleep well that night despite the medication I was given. It was not so much the dread of the surgery, as it was a progression of unrelated thoughts and feelings. I thought about all of the things never foreseen or intended that had happened to me over the last few years—about my marriage, Lisa, life and death, and about what had happened to me at Melodyland. What did it all mean?

Somehow, through the night, I gained the assurance that everything was going to be all right. Even my recovery time would be, I was sure, relatively easy. I couldn't have been more wrong—about that part, at least.

"Im sick to my stomach and so thirsty, please help me!"

I could hear voices off somewhere, and through the dim light and shadows, I could see someone, but my eyes were fuzzy and I wasn't sure. Then I heard a voice.

"No, you can't have anything to drink. You've been sick to your stomach for hours, and Dr. Marks left strict orders that you are to have nothing."

"Then I'll ask him myself," I retorted. She responded that it was three o'clock Saturday morning and I would have to wait until seven to talk to the doctor.

"Until then you are to have nothing. Dr. Marks is a real bugger about his patients drinking after surgery, because they get sick. And when he leaves an order, we follow it!"

Suddenly a woman screamed. I could hear a lot of banging. The nurse left my bedside in a rush. I could not focus my eyes and felt frustrated at not being able to orient myself. I cried out and a man asked if he could help. He said his wife was in the bed next to mine. She had just lost their baby in childbirth due to complications.

"Yes," I answered, "could you please give me a drink of water? I'm so thirsty I think I'm going to die. Please help me." Apparently he hadn't heard the nurse and he sweetly accommodated me. As the thirst momentarily passed, I became aware of the horrible pain I was in. Then I discovered I couldn't move because I was hooked up to so many things. Besides, I was one big bandage! The great thirst returned, and I asked my new-found friend for more water. After drinking this time, I was promptly sick to my stomach. While the nurse was helping me, there was again a scream and a great commotion in the room.

"Good Lord," I said aloud, "where do they have me? What's going on?"

"This is intensive care," the man who had given me water said, "and they have a girl in here who keeps having some kind of fit."

The screams, I later learned, were coming from a young woman who had formerly taken LSD. After oral surgery on Friday, she started having flashbacks and hallucinations as a result of the anesthesia. She was astonishingly strong, and would thrash about, banging her head on the bars. They had placed pillows all around the bed and finally had to tie her down. Even with that, she got so wild it took all of the personnel in the room to restrain her.

The nurse finally got back to clean me up. "I don't know where you're bringing this all up from. Your stomach should have been empty long ago." I didn't tell her I'd been drinking water, and a few minutes later I was thirsty again. In spite of the degrading prospect of being covered with my own vomit, I once more asked the gentleman for a drink of water. By now he realized what was happening and refused. But I talked him into letting me suck on an ice cube.

I was bleeding more profusely than normal for this type of surgery, and a nurse called the doctor for permission to give me a blood transfusion. I vomited again. Just as they came to clean me up and start the transfusion, the girl on the other side of the room began kicking and screaming again. All of the attendants in the room laid everything else aside to restrain her once more. This happened twice while they were trying to start my transfusion.

I was in the most severe pain I had ever felt. That, combined with the chaos reigning in the ward, convinced me I would never live to see daybreak. About 4:30, through my haziness I saw my husband walk through the door and over to my bedside. "I couldn't sleep," he said. "I had a feeling you needed me."

"Oh," I whispered, "thank you for coming. I need help. I think I'm going to die."

Arnold sized up the situation, and even though he was not on the staff of that hospital, he began to attend to my needs. He stayed a couple of hours, until my father walked in. Dad said, "Arnold, you'd better go home and get some rest. I'll stay here until you can come back."

Arnold kissed me. Tears filled his eyes. "I love you, Joni. Everything is going to be all right—wait and see."

Dad, too, had tears in his eyes. I said, "Dad, I feel so weak and I'm in so much pain. I don't know if I can make it or not."

"I know, kid, but you're strong. You'll make it."

When Dr. Marks came in that morning, dad said, "This place is a snake pit with all this screaming and turmoil. It's been like a nightmare for her." Dr. Marks quickly decided to move me to a private room, next to the nurses' station where I could be watched closely.

I was very ill. My hemoglobin count dropped to four, and I spent the next ten days having blood transfusions, shots, pills, drifting in and out of fitful sleep and crying out in pain. I was not allowed to have visitors, except for my immediate family, and a woman from the church who worked in the building next door. She came over every day to pray for me.

One day my Aunt Faith came in as I was having a transfusion. She took my hand and began to pray.

"I've been too weak and too doped up to pray," I whispered, "but through all of this hell I've been lying here saying, 'Thank you, Jesus, thank you.' "

She smiled. "That's a prayer, too." I closed my eyes. Because of the mighty hand of God alone, my life was spared. I was grateful.

As I regained some of my strength, I was allowed to have visitors—a few close friends. Jean walked into the room and gasped, "My gosh, girl, where did you get all of these flowers? I can hardly find you through this floral maze!"

"This is nothing," I commented. "You should see the flowers I've been sending down the hall to other rooms. Some came with clowns, balloons and cuddly toys attached. They've been sending them over to the pediatric ward."

"I didn't know you knew so many people, Joni."

"Neither did I," I laughed. "I don't understand it. Patients that come into Arnold's office in the evenings, after I'm gone, are sending flowers. People I have never heard of are sending flowers, letters and gifts. You'd think I was someone really important.

"By the way, Jean, I can't see well enough to focus my eyes because of the pain injections. Will you read the cards to me?"

After she had read them all, she commented on how lovely and encouraging they all were. Then, without preamble, she said, "Joni, aren't you just lying there saying, 'Why me?' "

"No," I answered honestly, "it hasn't occurred to me to think of it that way. Actually, I'm grateful to be alive." Then I proceeded to tell her of the exchange Dr. Marks and I had had a few days previous. He had stopped in on his morning rounds.

"How's my lucky patient this morning?"

"Lucky?" I asked skeptically.

"Yep, lucky! Remember me telling you it was virtually impossible to find this type of cancer at this stage?" I nodded. "I've had three pathologists ask me how I ever found it. I told them I didn't, that I have a crazy patient

101

who found it herself. Guess you have a lucky star someplace!''

I smiled. "Luck had nothing to do with it. The Lord in heaven was the little voice that kept telling me I had cancer.''

"Whatever you wish to call it, Joni, you're fortunate to be alive. The hospital pathologist said that if we were to put it on a scale of one to ten as to how close it was to being too late, you'd rate about a nine!''

As I related this to Jean, I was again awed by God's direct intervention in the course of my life. "I'll tell you, Jean, I breathed a sigh as I realized my heavenly Father had given me back my life. Dr. Marks said he was certain they had gotten all of the cancer and I was going to be all right.''

"Joni, that's beautiful,'' Jean murmured. "I'm so glad.''

I knew by her voice that she didn't yet perceive just what a miracle had happened to me.

"I'm leaving the hospital today,'' I happily told one of my favorite nurses. She was a robust person, and as jovial as anyone I had ever met.

"We'll miss you,'' Stella said. "You've been a good patient.'' I told her—as I had told anyone who would listen—about God revealing my cancer to me. She responded as though she knew what I was talking about. "I'll pray you will always be well. Now make yourself pretty for your husband and daughter. Here comes the doctor. It won't be long now.''

Dick took the dressings off. "You've been hollering for a bath—well, here it comes. I'm going to have the nurse take you down the hall to the tub, so you can bathe. You must promise me one thing, though," he said, becoming serious.

"What's that?"

"While you're down there, I want you to take a good look at yourself. You've kept your eyes closed during all the dressing changes, and I insist you look at yourself before leaving."

"I guess I'll have to sooner or later. May as well be now."

Stella helped me into a nice warm tub, and as she backed out the door she said, "Now honey, do what the doctor told you. And just remember, you're a pretty lady inside and out, and you always will be."

I smiled weakly as I sank down into the warm bubbly water. Stella was gone now and I felt afraid. What would I see—and what wouldn't I see? I obeyed orders. I glanced quickly at first, and then intently looked down at my chest. I screamed silently as my eyes beheld the yet fresh and gaping wound that went from under one arm to under the other. I was stunned, convinced I would never become accustomed to myself this way. The tub could have nearly overflowed with the tears I shed that morning. Grief and depression swept over me like a blanket, and I became angry with myself.

I should be happy, I told myself. I'm getting better. I'm alive and about to go home to my family. But lecture as I might, I remained inconsolable.

Back in my room, I was exhausted by the ordeal. I lay down on the bed to wait for Arnold and Lisa. I wanted to look calm and happy when they came. I hadn't seen Lisa since entering the hospital, and I was eager to be home again. Would they be long?

Arnold soon walked into the room—white and shaking. Lisa looked crushed, her eyes bloodshot from crying, a sob or two still rattling in her chest. She came over to the bed and hugged me. "Hi, mom, it sure is good to see you. Are you going to be all right?"

She was clinging more than hugging. "What's wrong, honey? Are *you* all right?"

She pulled away and shook her head, darting a glance at Arnold. "Nothing is wrong," she said stiffly.

Arnold's voice was tense as he said he would go down to the office and check me out. After he left, I again asked Lisa what was wrong. She started to cry.

"I can't tell you. Doc said he'd kill me if I talked to you about it."

I had a frantic feeling in the pit of my stomach but I tried to sound calm. "You know he'll do no such thing. Please tell me what's the matter—why do you look so hurt?"

"Well, Doc got mad at me this morning about something I said to Lenora. While he was bawling me out, he went on to tell me that he was now going to insist I call him dad instead of Doc. I told him I didn't feel like he was my dad, and I wasn't going to call him that. Then he yelled, 'I'd rather have you call me a bastard than to call me Doc!' He looked at me like he hated me. It scared me a lot."

My heart broke for them both, almost more than I could bear. I asked Arnold on the way home what was wrong, and he angrily gave me a short version of the same story.

I was already quite upset with Arnold over the way he had treated me in the hospital. His earnest concern had turned cold when it became apparent I was not going to die. He would come to see me quite late at night, usually after I had been sedated. It didn't matter, though. He had almost nothing to say to me and each visit depressed me a little more. My last two nights there we had actually argued about it.

After hearing Arnold tell about his bout with Lisa, I had become so upset that I was hysterical by the time we turned into our driveway.

"Why did you have to pick this day to fight with Lisa over such a subject?! I wasn't even through the front door before we were having problems again. I can't stand it!" I screamed, with a ferocity that startled me. "I don't want to be used as a pawn in your attempts to force Lisa to call you dad. As if that would really change things!"

I was once more confronted with the untenable situation with Arnold—nothing had changed. Not only my chest, but every fiber of my being was raw. I couldn't stop crying. "I needed to feel protected and loved today," I sobbed. Finally Arnold called Dick for some help. He prescribed a tranquilizer and some sleeping pills.

When we were getting ready for bed, Arnold said, "I think I'll sleep in the guest room. There are too many flowers in here, and besides, I'm afraid I might roll over in the night and bump you."

"Okay," I answered. "I don't sleep well yet anyway. I can't get comfortable. I feel like I've been hit in the chest by a Mack truck!"

Several nights later, I was doing better—and feeling lonesome. "Arnold, why don't you come back to bed with me? I'm sure you'd sleep better on our mattress. Besides, it'd be nice to be next to you again, and to be held a bit—carefully, of course," I laughed. But Arnold didn't laugh.

"I can't, Joni. Your condition is still too delicate, and I'd worry all night about bumping into you."

I felt I had been rejected. It was the final blow. As the weeks went on, I had a sense of mourning I couldn't shake. I mourned my mother, whom I missed terribly during my convalescence without all her help and loving concern. I mourned the loss of a part of my body. And I mourned for my marriage. Arnold never shared our bed with me again.

I began to wonder about returning to work. One day not long after the operation, I had occasion to call Arnold's office and I mentioned to the staffer who answered the extraordinary number of cards and flowers that had come from Arnold's patients.

"Well, I'm not surprised, Mrs. Harper," she said, "because just as soon as you went into the hospital, your husband put up a big sign in the waiting room that said, 'My wife has been stricken with the most dread disease ever to come upon mankind. Will you please encourage her with cards and letters.' And your husband got a lot of sympathy, too—some of it pretty affectionate!"

I was boiling, and it wasn't so much about his female patients. It was because Arnold's sweetness and generosity had fooled me too long. The truth was that I had married a man who was utterly self-centered. So when he asked me when I'd like to come back to work, my answer was guarded.

"I've enjoyed not having to rush off to work every morning. It gives me more time to spend with Lisa. Actually, I've been so busy with other things, I hadn't really thought about the office." What I didn't say was that since Arnold no longer treated me like a wife—avoiding me physically—I wasn't sure I wanted to help in the office any more.

"Well, I have mixed feelings too," he said. "It's been nice for you to be home, but things aren't the same when you're not at the office. I really need you there."

I think he sensed my real feelings. A few days later, we argued about it I had been seeing my psychiatrist again, who had recommended that I stay out of the practice and let Arnold take over the business end of it. "He said our marriage might be better," I concluded.

"Who are you going to listen to, him or me?" Then very angrily he shrugged his shoulders. "Oh, well, do whatever you want. I don't give a damn."

The way he backed down from a fight had always infuriated me more than anything else. In fury I screamed, "All I've ever been to you is a body and a business partner. Now that I'm neither, what's left for us? Why don't you just get out and leave me alone?"

That pretty much ended things. Or maybe it just ended the pretense. Arnold came home later and later at night and I got angrier and angrier. He always managed to fall asleep on the couch. Any closeness between us was gone.

I felt more alone than ever. Psychiatry was never going to be the answer, even though it had helped me get in touch with my feelings. I felt I had come to a dead end.

When I think back now on how God had spoken to me in such a dramatic way of His love and presence by revealing the cancer no one else would have found, the next events in my life astonish me.

7

"You've got to go to this woman. She's absolutely amazing! She told me things no one else could possibly know about me." Harriet's voice was full of wonder. She was one of Arnold's patients, and she had just come from a visit with a psychic. I was riveted to my seat as she described it.

"What did you say her name is? Do you think you could get me an appointment with her? And what about that male psychic you told me about awhile back? I've got to have some answers to my life."

In the past, Harriet and I had discussed current books we had both read on the subjects of reincarnation, ESP and similar interests. We were fascinated by the "spiritual world."

She had called me many times during and after my illness. We spent a lot of time comparing notes about our marital problems. She had recently had an astrological chart done and was trying to guide her days by it. She said it was helpful and suggested I think of having one done for myself.

"Joni, I've made an appointment with Sarah for you. It's very difficult to get in to see her, so be sure you keep it—and good luck!"

It was a hot and humid day in September that I drove off in my shiny, air-conditioned Mark IV. I told no one where I was going, except Jean, who shared my interest in the occult. We had talked on the phone that morning.

"I've not found any answers elsewhere. Maybe I will here. What do you think?" I asked Jean. Then, before she had a chance to respond, I added, "You know, I feel a little guilty. I don't know why I remember this, but somewhere in the Bible it says not to consult with fortune-tellers—something about it being an abomination to God." Somehow we managed to decide it didn't apply and off I went.

That first visit set a trend. Harriet knew of more than one psychic and so did Jean. If I didn't like what one would tell me, I'd run to another. I went to a tarot card reader, and to an astrologist who did psychic readings.

I occasionally opened the Bible, wondering what on earth people found so interesting in there. None of it made much sense to me, until one night, my eye fell upon a verse.

You have advisors by the ton—your astrologers and stargazers, who try to tell you what the future holds. But they are as useless as dried grass burning in the fire. They cannot even deliver themselves! You'll get no help from them at all. Theirs is no fire to sit beside to make you warm! (Isa. 47:13, 14, TLB)

I had some pangs of remorse, then, and one day I went to a counselor at my church.

"Do you think there's anything wrong with visiting psychics and astrologers?"

"I really don't know," she said, "but I don't think it can do any harm." I liked that—it was what I wanted to hear.

Arnold and I had begun marriage counseling with a psychiatrist. We were having some terrible arguments—it seemed the only way we could communicate by then. During one fight, Arnold looked at me with loathing.

"Get away from me! Don't you know yet how much you turn me off?"

I ran crying to the phone and called the doctor: "I can't stand it. I've got to talk to you."

"Well, I'm completely booked up, but if you can be here at 7:00 in the morning, I'll see you then."

How convenient, I thought. I had an appointment with a reader in the vicinity at 9:30. I could lump the two meetings together.

The visit with the psychiatrist was unusually satisfying, and I felt much comforted when I left his office. I was eager for my next appointment, and hurried to my car—where I found I had locked myself out. It had been pouring rain that morning and I had rushed out of my car to the doctor's office, intent only on keeping dry. As I surveyed my dilemma, two young men came over.

"Now how could a good lookin' woman like you do such a dumb thing? I've heard of dumb blondes, but never dumb redheads!"

They produced a coat hanger from a nearby business and

soon had my door unlocked amid much good humor and joking around. As I thanked them and was on my way, I could feel that this was going to be a day to remember!

I began driving down Wilshire Boulevard. The rain had turned to a drizzle, the early morning sunlight coming like silver through the soft mist. I reached for my sunglasses, which were on the adjacent seat, and when I couldn't find them by touch I looked over. When I turned my attention back on the road, it was too late.

I was driving through an intersection on a red light. Another car was approaching very fast, too fast to stop. The crash was sickening. My car went spinning. Inside it, I was being thrown from side to side. Then—I'll never forget it—I heard a voice speak as if it were in the car with me.

"Be still and know that I am God."

At last the car stopped. My ankle was throbbing painfully. The man in the other car was moaning loudly as they tried to get him in the waiting ambulance. A policeman came to the window of my car where I sat unable to get out because the door was caved in.

"Is he going to die?" I asked frantically.

"I don't know the extent of his injuries," the officer answered. "Right now, let's worry about getting you out of this car."

By this time, my ankle was so badly swollen I nearly panicked.

The gentleman I had hit and I were both taken to UCLA's emergency room. The morning rain had slickened the streets and there had been many accidents. All the examining rooms were full and I lay in the hall, asking every nurse who walked by if I might have something for pain. The answer was always the same: "There are no doctors available presently. We can give you nothing until one has examined you."

Finally I was treated and x-rayed. The doctor interrupted one of my groans. "You'll need more x-rays of this ankle in a few days after the swelling goes down. We can't tell much about it yet. You seem to be okay otherwise, except for the bruises."

"Thank God," I breathed. "How is the man I hit?"

"He has several fractured ribs, which gave him a lot of pain. But he'll survive in good shape."

The worst was apparently over. My thoughts went back to that voice I had heard right after the impact. I had been frightened and assured by it in the same moment. What did it mean? I couldn't come up with any profound answers, but the basic message was clear enough. I never went to another fortuneteller or soothsayer of any kind after that.

Arnold walked in, looking stern. I wasn't eager to see him. I was afraid he'd ask me where I'd been going.

"Joni, what next?"

"Don't you care how I am?"

"Yes, of course I do. I can see you're not doing too well. Tell me how it happened."

Leaving UCLA, Arnold was very kind—outwardly. But I could feel how angry he was underneath. I began to sob.

"I hurt, Arnold, I hurt. Do you care that I'm hurting?"

He pulled the car onto the shoulder of the freeway and took my hand. He just looked at me.

"The physical pain is horrible," I cried, "but I'm talking about another kind of pain. I hurt on the inside more than I can stand. I don't want to hurt any more."

"I know you hurt," Arnold answered sadly, "and I don't know what to do about it."

"Joan, dear," Aunt Faith's sweet voice came over the telephone, "I can't bear knowing what you are going through. If you can stand the drive, why don't you come to Melodyland Thursday morning for the healing service? Maybe God will touch your ankle."

I thought the chance my ankle would be instantly, miraculously healed was very remote. I just accepted that I had to bear the consequences of what I'd brought upon myself. But the mental anguish of my meaningless daily existence *was* too much for me.

I had found that God will reach down and touch a life. He'd saved my life, and I was gradually coming to the realization that if He cared that much, He must have some purpose, some better direction for my life. He must have something in mind for me, I thought. I wanted that better life, and I was finally prepared to find it on His terms. I went to Melodyland that Thursday.

"Any of you who are lost and lonely and hurting, those who can say, 'I need God, I need answers to life's problems,' stand up right now and acknowledge your Savior: Jesus Christ."

It was as if Pastor Wilkerson was speaking directly to me. Whatever doubts I had that God had the answers I was seeking were swept away by what I heard as an appeal from God himself to me. In the crowded auditorium, I suddenly felt alone in the tremendous, and yet intimate, presence of the Lord. My heart was pounding and my voice quavering as I asked His forgiveness for having gone my own way without Him. And as I invited Jesus to be the

Lord over my life, I felt Him fill my heart with a peace that quieted my questions and stilled the storm in my soul. For the first time since I could remember, I felt steady and full of hope for my future.

I began attending these services regularly. In the back of my mind was the hope that one day Arnold would want to come with me. I wondered if I shouldn't stop seeing the psychiatrist. At our next joint session with him, Arnold spoke of a separation.

"She has told me enough times to get out if I wasn't happy—and I'm not happy." The doctor encouraged him to stay at least a few more weeks until I was more fully recovered from the accident, and also to give us a chance to work out some of his feelings through therapy. Later that evening, we had another argument, and it seemed to be the last straw for Arnold.

"This is it, Joni. I can't think straight around this place any more. I'm getting out." He packed up some of his things, loaded his car, and said, "I'll get some of my other things later—call you in a few days." With that, he spun out of the driveway and down the street.

As the sound of his car receded in the distance, I hoped he would cool off and come back. I listened for him all evening, assuring Lisa that everything was going to be all right. He called to say good night to Lisa—but not to me.

I tried to be philosophical: Well, here you are, alone again. But this time I wasn't just alone. I was more confused than I'd ever been, and I was physically and emotionally at the end of my resources. In the days that followed, I couldn't eat, sleep or think. I moved like a robot, doing routine chores as though I were in some kind of dream. I felt as if I was outside my body, watching things happen to me.

One question haunted me: why was I constantly on a crash course with failure? I had spent my lifetime going from one person to another, demanding love and total commitment, all the while convinced I wasn't good enough to have what I so desperately wanted.

My aunt had given me copies of two books, *Prison to Praise* and *Power in Praise*. I now read them with delight and excitement. They told of a new dynamic for one's life—praising God in every situation, whether good or bad. I knew nothing of the practice of praise the author described, or of the baptism in the Holy Spirit that he spoke of so glowingly. I wasn't sure I believed everything he said. But there was something there, and I wanted to know more about it.

I began to speak to people from my church about it. Some knew nothing and others said nothing. Finally I asked a friend who was a deaconess at the church if she had ever heard of the baptism in the Holy Spirit. Her face came to life.

"Amazing you should ask now," Betty replied. "Oh, Joni, yes! I've been baptized in the Holy Spirit and I speak with other tongues." She said she thought this was a gift God wanted all His people to have. "There is a power for living in this, Joni, and love—oh, the love for others I feel since it happened is amazing. I don't talk about it at the church, though. It's kind of controversial."

Excitement welled up within me. "Betty, where did you learn about all of this? How did it happen?"

She told me she had met a couple, George and Virginia Otis, who had been having Bible studies in their home. She attended for quite a while, and one night she asked them to

116

pray for her. That was when she received the Holy Spirit. Betty looked at me lovingly.

"When you're feeling stronger, I want to have you over for lunch. I have some close friends whom I met at the Otis's, and these gals have all had this same experience. They'd love to meet you, and I'm sure you'll find what they have to say very interesting."

Several weeks later the luncheon took place, and I met Rosemary and her two married daughters, Andrea and Lynn. They mentioned belonging to a little church on Sherman Way in Van Nuys called "The Church on the Way." They were lovely people and I felt their genuine concern for me. After lunch, Andrea asked, "Joan, would you like for us to pray with you to receive the baptism?" I said I would.

Rosemary commented, "Andrea, I sense Joan is shy about this matter. Why don't you take her into the other room and talk awhile in private?" She was right! I was not used to praying aloud with people. So Andrea talked to me for quite a while and then prayed with me. I felt the Lord's presence, but nothing out of the ordinary happened.

"Thanks for taking your time with me, Andrea, but I guess I'm not ready."

As I left, disappointed and confused, the women waved good-by, and I heard one of them say, "Come visit Church on the Way sometime—we have prayer services at 7:30 Wednesday nights."

Arnold had been gone for several weeks and we had little communication. One night, after Lisa had gone to bed, my feelings of loneliness seemed to claw, terrifyingly, at my mind. In my bedroom, behind closed doors, curled up in a ball on the floor, I wept. I cried for my yesterdays and my tomorrows. I sat with my arms wrapped around my knees like an abandoned child, rocking back and forth.

"God, God, please help me. You spoke audibly to me. You revealed cancer to me. If these things have really been you, I need to hear from you again. I need a miracle in my life and I need it now, or I can't go on!"

Suddenly I thought of a tape I had, a reading of some of the more comforting Psalms. I had given the tape to Jean many months before when she was having troubles. Yesterday she had remarked, "Joni, I don't know what to do to help you, but do you remember that tape you gave me? It was such a comfort right then."

After my plea to God, I didn't feel different, but I got into bed and played the tape over and over again. I listened half the night, and I was greatly comforted as the healing power of God's Word spread through my being. I had never paid much attention to the Bible before. I wondered if God had permitted some of my circumstances to bring me to a better understanding of myself.

I played the lovely tape night and day for several days, and in the reassuring words from God himself I heard for the first time a message of the reality of God and His presence with me. A certainty was born in my heart that He would not fail me now.

Although I lived seventy miles from Melodyland, I began to regularly attend the Thursday and Sunday morning services, many times spending all of Sunday there so I could attend the evening service also. The 140-mile round trip did not seem far at all. Even the labyrinth of early morning traffic across the Santa Ana

Freeway didn't faze me. I was starved, empty, and ready to be filled. I was seeing the Book of Acts in the Bible in action, watching miracles happen, seeing people give of themselves to one another, and feeling the love of God all around me. I abruptly discontinued my visits with the doctor, for I knew I was on my way to a real healing of the heart and mind.

Melodyland has a large bookstore, and I spent a great deal of time browsing there. I discovered and read such books as *They Speak with Other Tongues, Aglow with the Spirit, Nine O'Clock in the Morning* and *A New Song.* How excited I became, how desirous to receive the experience they all described—the baptism in the Holy Spirit with all of its joys and its healing impact in one's life.

Aunt Faith and I were enjoying a few minutes in the bookstore one day when I picked up a book.

"I like this man's face. *High Adventure!* Hmm, I could use some high adventure right now—think I'll buy it." Aunt Faith laughed.

"Dear, do you mean there is a book left here you haven't read yet?"

"Well, there's this one, and the name seems familiar somehow, so why not?"

It was a beautiful, balmy April afternoon in Hidden Hills. The sparkling pool, blue under the afternoon sun, beckoned to me. I dove in, and afterwards, with a big frosty glass of iced tea, I took the plunge into George Otis's book that was to change my life.

I read all afternoon, fascinated. I laughed and cried, reading and rereading, practically memorizing the pages.

There were tremendous parallels I could relate to. Although Arnold and I had not reached the pinnacle of success that George Otis had, we had known our share. At many points I could identify with the feelings he described. I thought, "I'm not the only one with such a vast emptiness on the inside. His has been filled and mine will be too." I sensed I was on the verge of something new and exciting. Little did I know how direct and personal George Otis's impact would be on my life during the coming months.

But these days were some of my most tormenting. I wanted desperately for my life to be put back together. I wanted to find all the pieces, and I hoped God would put each in its perfect place.

That week all my fears and doubts reached a peak. By Wednesday my insides felt like they'd been turned inside out, and I wondered if I'd last until the next morning's prayer meeting at Melodyland. Lisa asked why I was so restless and agitated.

"I've just got to get with God's people and feel His presence, now!" I exclaimed, surprising myself with my vehemence. Then I recalled the Wednesday night prayer meeting at that "little church" on Sherman Way that I'd heard about at Betty's luncheon. That evening I drove the twenty miles into Van Nuys; it was to mark the beginning of something entirely new.

When I walked into the plain, chapel-like sanctuary of The Church on the Way, I immediately sensed a mood I never would have expected. There was an intimacy like that between brothers and sisters—it was love. And gladness. As I watched people talk and smile, and shyly shook the hands offered me in greeting, an optimism began to lift the heaviness in my heart. I looked into faces that were both relaxed and excited. They knew they did not have to compromise, they believed their needs would be met. I felt it myself, that curious feeling of fulfillment before the fact.

When these people sang, the room was filled with their joy. They sang simple songs with lyrics I recognized as verses from the Bible. All over, people in front of me, the two persons on either side, and probably (I dreaded to look) everyone behind were raising their hands in utter abandonment. It looked like mass surrender, and I felt I'd be picked out of the crowd at any moment for clasping my hands calmly in front of me. It was with as much relief as astonishment that I heard the pastor, Jack Hayford, characterize my discomfort exactly.

He struck me as a man who had all the presence of a gifted performer, this in spite of himself. He was tall, of average build, with a crest of baldness rising out of a fringe of brown hair. His eyes were small and closely set, and their look was extraordinary. They seemed to see far into a realm I'd never seen before, and their penetrating, constantly moving gaze took in all of us, each of us. He radiated energy and a vitality that made me feel like I'd just then begun to live.

"Welcome," he began, leaning into the word as if he were talking to a neighbor who'd ambled into his back yard. "If this is your first time at The Church on the Way, I want to reassure you," raising his hand as if to stop our worst fears, "if you've been able to handle it so far, it doesn't get any worse." From the delighted laughter that erupted everywhere, I understood that most of the people there had at one time felt as I did—including their pastor. I liked him already.

"We don't mean to sound smug or arrogant about what goes on around here," he said dryly, as if he couldn't stand the taste of that thought. He seemed to scan the congregation for anyone who might be offended, and his voice softened. "We realize there are some people who might be disturbed by the differences in our services from what they're used to. I think you'll find there's a sanity in what we do, and a sincere desire to worship God." He slowly moved off the platform and toward us, mingling with the congregation.

"Our objective here is that everyone grow in the knowledge and love of the Lord. His truth will make you free." He spoke simply, liltingly, his hands sculpting the words in the air as if to give them form and shape. "And this is following Jesus. And He's the Lord. We talk about Him quite a bit. We're interested in following the will of God. Anyone who knows anything about the love of God toward them has become aware that He has a specific design for their life.

"And since that is so, it is our responsibility to grow in the knowledge of the Lord and to walk in His way. And that's what we're going to talk about tonight. How do you see the Lord's way when everything around you seems to be a dead-end street?" I caught my breath, suddenly seeing in my mind's eye the little church I'd glimpsed just before smashing into the telephone pole so many years ago on the dead-end street. The light in the pastor's face as he turned in my direction made my heart leap into my throat.

"My brother and sister," he addressed us tenderly, "if you're here tonight and you feel you're on a dead-end street, and you say, 'Lord, I don't understand, I'm hurting, or I'm broke; my marriage is a battleground; I've had an abortion; I've got a terrible temper; I'm divorced; I'm afraid of what tomorrow has for me,' He will say, 'Let me show you so you'll understand.' "

As I listened to that list, I felt my heart constrict with the pain of memories. Then, at his last words, the ice that had closed off my soul cracked, and light poured in through the fissure. Tears coursed down my cheeks, but I was not crying for myself.

"There's something you can't see working out the way you'd like. If you'll listen to the Lord, He will draw you to himself and so catch you up that you will know with a settled certainty that God will not fail you."

I was crying because I recognized God—my God. He was more noble, more compassionate, more holy than I had ever imagined; He was more faithful to me than any human being had ever been or would ever be. And like the father I had only been able to dream about having, His voice filled my heart: "You're home."

As Pastor Jack spoke, his words seemed to merge with that voice and I listened to God as He showed me the meaning of the most profoundly mysterious and violent turn my life had taken.

"I'm going to tell you—any outworking of God's purpose in you and me at one point or another is going to start cutting into the flesh of your life. It's not the Lord leading you to a suffering, agonizing misery. It's just that there is so much outcropping, disfiguring flesh that needs to be carved off so we'll fit through the doorway of where He wants us to go." I knew in these striking, almost brutal images, he was speaking of the damage to the personality done by sin.

"God's got a pruning job to do. Not with an ounce of

intent to injure you do those shears cut. You sure feel their sharpness. But the Father knows how to do a pruning job that guarantees increased fruit appearing without the tree bleeding to death. It's going to survive the treatment. God is saying to you, dear ones, 'Everything of my way results from this cutting, this sacrifice.' "

Sitting there, I felt that time had stopped, as God patiently explained how He'd pursued me with His love. What I had thought was the destruction of my womanhood, my mastectomy, had been allowed as a literal pruning of my physical life so that spiritual life could begin and bear fruit. I saw that indeed I had not been left hurting and bleeding to death, I was actually more whole than I had ever been. This was the way my Lord chose to stop me in my headlong tracks, to show me himself, to teach me of His ways to man.

I knew then, without a shadow of a doubt, that I wouldn't want my body the way it was if it meant having the soul I had, a soul that did not know God. In that moment, I accepted myself as I was, and blessed this dear God, my Lord, for cherishing me so. I wept with joy and with a release that freed my very bones. He had opened the prison of my past failures at being a woman. I was His daughter, as beautiful as He had always intended me to be. I was more of a woman than I had ever been. I smiled then.

"I'm still me."

About a week earlier I had heard from Arnold. "Hi, hon, how are you?" Not having heard from him in several weeks, I was surprised, but I tried not to let him hear it.

"I'm doing better," was all I could manage. Up to now, we had spoken neither of a divorce nor of my wish to stay together. I held my breath, waiting to hear what he had called to say.

"Remember Alexis, my patient who works for a cruise line?"

"Yes, I remember her well," I nearly whispered, fearing what he was going to say next.

"Well, she's involved in some public relations for the line and has offered us a free cruise to Acapulco. Would you like to go? Maybe it will do us both good to get away together. Perhaps we could come to some conclusions about our difficulties. What do you think? I need to know in a couple of weeks."

"I don't know what to say. Please give me some time to think this over." His voice softened a bit as he promised to call the following week.

I tried to pray about the trip to Acapulco, but I got more confused as each day came and went. I needed guidance, but from whom? I had left my church of ten years; I hadn't been attending Melodyland long enough to feel free to contact their staff; and I didn't have the faintest idea who to approach at Church on the Way.

I had never in my life done as much as write a fan letter, a letter to an editor or a public official. But suddenly I thought of George Otis and *High Adventure*. Contrary to all my natural reticence, I decided to try to seek his counsel. I recalled that in the book he had mentioned his ministry, Bible Voice, which was in Van Nuys. I looked up the number and dialed, half-expecting a rebuff. The voice on the other end said, "Mr. Otis is out of town this week, but if it's urgent I'll give you their home phone number and you can speak with Mrs. Otis." Bingo, I thought. "Yes, that will be fine. Please give me that number."

Virginia Otis listened quietly at the other end as I told her of reading her husband's book and gave her a thumbnail sketch of myself and my problem. I told her I was desperately in need of spiritual counsel, and felt they were the people who could help me.

"I feel so foolish," I commented. "I've never done anything like this before!"

"Well, if you think about it," Virginia reassured me, "the Lord often had people do things that seemed foolish—just before doing something great!" That put my mind at ease. She went on. "I believe God is in this because no one ever gives out our home number at the office. I don't know how that happened, but I'm glad it did. George will be speaking at a church in Van Nuys this coming Sunday evening. Do you know where The Church on the Way is?"

"Do I ever! I started going a few weeks ago and I just love it!"

"Joni, meet us after the service and George and I will talk with you. I'll be wearing a pink-and-white print dress, and I'll be sitting near the back. Look for me after the service."

I lived through the remainder of the week in a state of excited anticipation. I felt God *was* in it, and that our meeting on Easter Sunday would be a turning point for me.

That evening I found Virginia without difficulty, and we talked a bit while waiting for George. When he joined us, he greeted me with an enthusiasm that seemed to come naturally from his vibrant, dynamic personality. Because of the crowd milling around, he suggested we go to their car to talk. As we walked to the car, there was a tremendous air of expectation, and I knew something significant was about to happen.

George and Virginia were most patient with their time, as I described the circumstances of my life and the trip Arnold had asked me to take with him.

"Joan," George said, "I feel the Holy Spirit directing me to tell you some things. Because Arnold is still your husband, and has requested that you go, you should be submissive to his desires. Each day of that trip, let the love of God show through you, and we will pray God will direct your steps." He looked at me as if there were something else on his mind.

"Have you been baptized in the Holy Spirit yet, Joan?"

"No, but I want to be; oh, I want to be!"

"Then let's get about the Father's business!" he cheerfully replied.

George and Virginia both laid their hands on me and began to pray. At this point, it was as though I was being shut in, alone with Jesus. I knew He wanted to do something for me. I wanted to yield, but I didn't know how. For an instant I was frightened. I could no longer hear the words they were praying. George put his hand on my forehead.

"Satan, in the name of Jesus whose blood was shed for this child, I command you to loose her this instant!"

Electricity seemed to go through my body, and I began to shake and sob. They continued to pray. I felt the peace of Jesus settling in my heart.

"Speak out, Joan. The Holy Spirit has just come upon you."

A few words at first—then a few more, words I'd never heard before. I'd opened my mouth to praise God, and a new language was on my tongue. I was grateful for the words God gave me to speak. Tears mixed with joyous laughter. The Otises rejoiced with me, and sent me on my way saying, "Be sure and call us when you get back. We want to know how things go for you."

I used my new language all the way home, saying over and over again, "Thank you, Jesus, thank you." I couldn't stop crying and I didn't want to stop laughing. I felt loved and cleansed and put together for the first time in many years. How exciting it was that the Lord chose Easter Sunday to give me His special gift.

When I walked in the door, Lisa took one good look at me.

"What happened to you?"

I hadn't anticipated her question. I'd been so immersed in my new experience, I hadn't considered there might be a need to explain it.

"Jesus baptized me with His Holy Spirit, like the Bible says He does." Then I added thoughtfully, "I feel like a new person. I'd been wanting more of God, but I didn't know this was what I needed. I feel His love and power, and He's given me a new way to praise Him. It's a language I can't describe."

"Well, you certainly look different, but I really don't understand what you're talking about." I was confident she would, and soon.

"You will, honey; you will."

I contained my longing to be alone with God as best I could until Lisa went to bed. Then I knelt at my bedside and praised Him and prayed in my new-found language, far into the night. The words of Psalm 86 went through my mind, "In the day of my trouble I will call upon thee, for thou wilt answer me.'' What a wonderful answer He had given me! Little did I knew then that some of my battles had only begun, and the power of the Lord that I felt would be the strength to fight the battles that were ahead of me.

8

The plane had not yet taken off when Arnold fell fast asleep. When he was awakened by the stewardess asking if he wanted lunch, he looked over at me and I gave him a withering look.

"We've hardly talked in two-and-a-half months, Arnold. Couldn't you have stayed awake for a while? This isn't how I thought things were going to be."

"I'm tired, Joni. This is supposed to be a vacation and I do intend to rest."

From then on, our communication was minimal, and as the days wore on, we saw very little of each other. I read and sunned, and he pursued the ship's many activities. The lovely ports, the warm romantic nights, and the couples having the time of their lives with each other only made me feel more alone. The possibility that we could make some headway in straightening out our lives was the trip's one redeeming feature.

"I don't know how you're feeling or where you're

coming from," I said one evening, broaching the subject of our relationship. "Can't we talk, perhaps make some decisions?"

"I'm tired of the whole thing. I'm tired of talking, and I'm tired of you always having to hash things over. I don't have anything to say." I was exasperated.

"That's typical, Arnold. You're still unable to face up to a possible confrontation. Why can't you commit yourself to me in a simple verbal exchange? Why are you always running away?"

"Let's go eat, Joni," he said tiredly. "They've already announced our sitting twice." It was my turn to do the running.

"You go ahead—I'm not hungry. I'm going to bed," I said.

I read for a while before crying myself to sleep, as I had done many other nights. I regretted not going with Arnold, and I hated seeing that I was still the same as I'd always been. I thought I'd be different after that evening with the Otises. Because I had the Holy Spirit, and because I had prayed, I had expected God to somehow override my imperfections. I was becoming dimly aware that my insecurities, my old habits, and my pride would not disappear overnight. God wanted to participate in my life, not run it for me. He wanted to change me from the inside, and the healing of my personality was a lifelong prospect. But for right now, I just didn't know where to draw the line between my responsibility and God's enabling grace.

We arrived in Los Angeles, and drove home in unbroken silence. At the house, Arnold said, "I'll come over tomorrow night to talk to you about my coming back home." I spoke before I thought.

"I don't think I want you to come home. This trip has shown me how impossible we are together."

"Well, I'm coming anyway; so look for me."

He didn't show up and a door in my life closed that night. Arnold stopped calling us, and we didn't see him for eight months, when he dropped off a Christmas gift for Lisa. I began to settle into life without him, and I knew it had to be a different kind of life.

I immersed myself in The Church on the Way; there I was finding out what life was all about. The Bible, we were taught, is the whole counsel of God, a thorough guide to show us how to manage our everyday affairs and live our lives successfully. We were encouraged to read the Bible regularly and believe it, all of it. How relieved I was to find that God is a practical, as well as a spiritual, God. He's concerned about my daily well-being, not just where I'll spend eternity. His words are intended to produce life here and now, and in them He has a personal revelation of himself and His plans for each of us. I was excited to get to know my heavenly Father in this way.

All of the sermons given by the pastor were available on cassette tapes. I bought those recorded before I had begun to attend—nearly a hundred tapes. I purchased books by the boxful, and spent all my time either listening or reading. When I was working in the house or the yard, I had the tape recorder going. I traveled the freeways with the articulate voice of Jack Hayford for company.

I went back to the very beginning of the Bible and as I traced the unraveling of God's vast plan for man, I glimpsed a pattern for my own life. I came to understand that as a child of God, the Bible was as much my history as it was the history of the Israelites. His promises to them held good for me. He was the same God.

I saw the regret for my wasted years without Him dissipate in the face of a marvelous promise: "I will restore to you the years that the locust hath eaten" (Joel 2:25), the locusts of pride and fear. I had a destiny, given to me by a Father at the expense of His own Son's life. He exchanged Jesus' death for mine; because He lives, so could I. I was important to the most important Person of all! My Lord Jesus was the center of my life, and life *was* good. More than anything, I wanted to learn obedience and devotion to Him. I wanted to be as faithful to Him as He was to me.

There was real power in God's Word going forth in our home day and night, and I sensed that life was beginning again. Hope rose up within me, and my wounds began to heal. And it began to have its effect on Lisa as well.

Lisa had always gone to Sunday school, but during the two years prior to my going to Melodyland, she attended with reluctance. She had since gone with me to Melodyland and to The Church on the Way a few times, but hadn't known what to make of the services with respect to what she was used to. She was amazed at the things that were happening to me, and because of my insatiable appetite for tapes, records, books and Christian radio stations, she thought I had gone a little goofy. Lisa would walk in the door to the now familiar sound of Pastor Jack, flash a look at me, and flee to her room with a "Mom, not again!"

One night at Melodyland we heard a young evangelist, named Mario Murillo, preach. His directness and biting humor, coupled with genuine warmth and love, fascinated Lisa. As we left that evening she declared, "Boy, he's great! I want to come out here the next time he speaks. He was all over that platform. No wonder they call him the Mexican Jumping Bean!''

The following month at Lisa's suggestion we drove out to hear him again. That evening his message was primarily to people of Lisa's age, and at the close he extended an invitation to the young people: "If you want to make some kind of commitment to follow God, to experience His power in your lives, come forward.''

Lisa literally jumped out of her seat and went to the front of the platform, which is the stage of what was once a theater in the round. The stage, the stairs leading to it and the aisles filled with young people. The presence of God was unmistakable, as Mario led a powerful prayer for these kids

As the crowd dispersed, Lisa, with tears in her eyes, ran up the aisle and rushed over to me.

"It's happened, it's happened!" Yes, *it* had happened. She had been gloriously filled to overflowing with the Holy Spirit.

What followed was a real growth spurt in Lisa's life, a time of healing as she opened up to the Holy Spirit's ministry. She began to make new friends at church and school. She often freely told me she loved me, and I'd see her and her friends hugging one another in church in a gesture of their affection.

I too began to feel the power of love in my life. I quickly learned an important lesson. People do care. They care about you, and about what happens to you. They will stand with you in the midst of troubles and give of themselves when necessary.

As I learned how much others care, I began to care about

myself, and about other people. I had never felt like this toward others. I knew then that I had never loved before. It was a cold thought and it made me shudder. I had always tried to manipulate those I was close to, to win their affection. I never saw their needs; I didn't know how. I was saddened as I looked back and saw the person I could have been. Now I wanted to be that person.

I prayed, "Lord, show me—me. Reveal the things I need to know about me that keep me from being the woman you want me to be." He knew I couldn't stand to see it all at once, so He was gentle with me, recalling a little at a time the things from my past I had done. Some things I had not even thought were wrong. As I saw them, I asked Him to forgive me, and to cleanse my heart and fill it with love.

That summer the church offered a class on Bible principles for marriage and child rearing. I felt prompted to go. What I learned there about a healthy marriage destroyed all my illusions.

Until now, I thought I had been a pretty good wife to Arnold, and I couldn't understand why he had done the things he did. I believed absolutely that he had left me because he couldn't handle my mastectomy.

For the first time I saw that I too had been responsible for the wreck of our marriage. I saw how I had undermined my husband's self-respect. Self-righteous and critical, I had been utterly self-centered, all the while thinking I was a selfless person.

I knew if I never saw my husband again, I still had to tell him how wrong I had been, and ask his forgiveness. I wrote Arnold a letter telling all of this and asking his forgiveness, saying, "I believe God could still heal our marriage beyond all expectations." This was the first of several letters I wrote to him that summer, but he never acknowledged any of them.

Towards the end of the summer, I attended a week of seminars at Melodyland. The last day of the meetings Elmer and Lee Bueno, missionaries to South America, were ministering in song and teaching. They described how they had come to Melodyland with heavy hearts, burdened with the weight of disappointment in their marriage. They had built up false expectations for one another. They felt defeated and resentful. Jesus showed them that their marriage was just as important as the work He gave them to do. They asked God to make their marriage new, and He knocked down the barriers they had erected. They wanted to minister to others what God had given them—release from bitterness and hostility.

Elmer's voice seemed to speak directly to me. "Anyone wanting to be delivered from a root of bitterness, please come forward and allow us to pray for you. You can be set free in an instant." I knew I still had much bitterness and unforgiveness left in me towards Arnold, which had built up over the years, and surfaced with the memories.

I walked down the aisle and knelt on the stairs with many others. The Buenos were praying and laying hands on some of the people. Although no one so much as touched me, I began to weep uncontrollably, saying to God, "I give it all up to you, Father. I don't want to carry this bitter load any longer. Lord, release me now in Jesus' name!"

I felt a heavy weight leave my shoulders. I had been instantly and miraculously healed of the feelings toward

Arnold that I had carried around for years. I was free!

I had written a note to George and Virginia Otis as they had asked, and thanked them for their ministry to me. A few days later Virginia called me.

"Hello, Joni! We received your letter, and George would like to see you next week. We want to pray with you and Lisa regarding any residual problems you might be having from those things you mentioned." In my note I had talked about some of my experiences with the occult and hypnosis. "Will you come for prayer?"

"Of course! I'll look forward to it. I sure appreciate your interest in us."

I know there is a devil, and that he is a very real adversary that everyone must come to grips with. But the thought that he might have some kind of hold on me or Lisa was disconcerting. I didn't like to think he could take my past mistakes and make trouble for me now.

George carefully explained that dabbling in the occult or hypnosis opened doors for Satan's presence in our lives, which meant we were vulnerable to attacks that could disable us to walk freely in the way God intended. He prayed that Lisa and I would be freed from any spiritual oppression resulting from my participation in these things. He prayed for the healing power of the Holy Spirit to purify our minds and emotions.

After praying with both of us, George turned to me. "I feel the Lord wants you to know He is pleased with you for having pursued His will and His way. Jesus has made a tremendous difference in your life in a very short time. You've opened yourself to the Holy Spirit's ministry, and you've been filled with God's joy and peace and love. But now it's time to grow. You're not a spiritual babe any more. To grow you've got to give away what you've been given. You can't just be a hearer of the Word, you must be a doer. Jesus is asking you to trust Him and give, really give of yourself to others. He's ready if you are."

I immediately thought of what the Lord had shown me that morning. I had been lying in bed, praising God and thanking Him for another day of life, when a thought seemed to be crowding everything else out of my mind. As I listened, I became aware that the Lord was sharing His thoughts with me. Later that day I shared the impression with my best friend, Jean. She had received the Lord three months earlier. Since that time, He had completely changed her life, and our friendship had become really precious to me.

"I believe the Lord showed me something really exciting this morning, Jean."

"Well, good grief, girl, don't keep me in suspense. Let's hear it!"

"I feel the Lord told me I'll soon be going to work in a job I didn't seek, a job clearly given to me by Him."

"You mean you're not going to have to go knocking on doors looking? God is going to just drop a job in your lap?"

"That's right, and soon, too."

I thought this all over with some consternation. I wondered what George was really telling me. I had become quite content with the pattern of my new life and I wasn't sure I was ready for anything else. I decided not to worry, but just to wait and be open to whatever it was God wanted to do with my life.

About this same time, God began to deepen my commitment to The Church on the Way. More and more, I felt as though this was my spiritual home. There were some adjustments I had to make. For one, there was a feature of the services called ministry time. I called it "panic time."

If I'd have known that at some point in the service that first night we'd be called upon to make circles of three or four, share our personal needs with strangers, and then pray, one for another, out loud, I never would have crossed the threshold. It wasn't much easier now. I'd stand there with sweating palms and shaking knees, wondering what on earth I was doing there, just wishing the floor would open up and swallow me. "It's time to crawl under the seat now," Lisa would mutter.

At first I chalked it off to shyness. But as I yielded to the idea that God wants His people to be honest and transparent, and to give of themselves, I realized I was laboring with pride. I was so absorbed in what others might think about me. I didn't want to feel or look foolish. I depended on their good opinion of me, and didn't want to admit I had needs. As I joined with others in small prayer circles, I was confronted by the pride I felt in being able to do everything on my own. In the discomfort I felt in these circles, I glimpsed the roots of my self-sufficiency. My supposed independence stemmed from a deep-seated fear. It was my defense against the rejection and hurt I had experienced ever since my childhood. But as I faced people at this personal level week in and week out, something dynamic and gentle began to happen inside of me.

I found I could be weak in the midst of others, and still

be accepted. It seemed that with every visit to the church, I couldn't outgrow my surprise at these people's willingness to accept me as I was. It was both lovely and strange to no longer feel the necessity to perform, or to struggle for attention and approval.

As I kept coming to the church, I recognized Jesus was changing not only my life, but that of many others. These times of personal praying and sharing with and for each other really exploded my concepts about God and His people. As we stood there with our hands joined together, praying to our Lord to meet our specific needs, I sensed a miracle was happening. We were exhibiting a child-like simplicity I knew most of us as adults were not capable of on our own. As we worshiped God and desired to know Him, it became more natural to care about others. There was a delicious sense of genuineness about the whole thing.

We were finding (much to everyone's amazement, I think) that God had created us to really need one another. From the Bible we were being taught that Jesus builds His church like a physical body whose differing parts are all equally essential and work together in harmony. As we studied God's Word, the Holy Spirit was confirming what we learned through our experience together as a church body. God was encouraging us to see ourselves as His family, a family of believers wedded together in His Son.

This was the larger view of what we were learning. Like any family, we had our moments. Prayer circles seemed to be the crucible wherein dust and deity came together. No matter how often I'd done it before, I could still feel painfully awkward when it came time to share my prayer requests. Even so, I appreciated the pressure. I soon learned we were all equally vulnerable. This was aptly characterized for me one day.

Jean and I were in a service together and were nearing the time of sharing. She leaned over and whispered, "Sometimes I feel like such a dope when we do this. I wish I were exempt or something. Sometimes I actually feel like I have something to say, but I don't know how to say it." I immediately thought of a Scripture that had really spoken to me a few days before.

"I have just the Scripture to help you!" I confidently said, whipping out my Bible (with which I was not too familiar yet) to show her Numbers 22:38: "The word that God putteth in my mouth, that shall I speak."

"Look, here it is," and together we read, "And the Lord opened the mouth of the ass." I had stopped ten verses too soon. I decided right then if I wanted to fit in with the family, I had better become more familiar with God's Word.

Pastor Jack was a true inspiration during this time of adjustment. He would render his own shortcomings in refreshingly frank, technicolor stories that left you in tears of laughter—or was it tears of joy that like him, you could also take off your mask and still be accepted? At other times, his own integrity led him to solemnly confess his mistakes and his faults before the congregation, and ask our forgiveness. He taught us all how to be real.

In fact, he redefined reality in God's terms. Each of his messages was a revelation to me, as his passion for God's Word, the sum of his experience and his personal integrity combined to give me life-changing insights into Scripture. He was dedicated to that. As our pastor, he was committed to our reaching our highest potential as sons and daughters of the Lord. The depth of his love and guidance was dramatically illustrated to me one Sunday.

"Mom, I miss Doc this morning. It's close to my birthday and I was thinking about how he won't be here to share it with me," Lisa was saying, with jumbo tears about to spill over. We were on our way to church. During sharing time Pastor Jack came over to us and spoke to Lisa.

"You're not lookin' too happy this morning, what's the problem?" She told him what she had told me. Jack's heart went out to her. He opened his Bible to Psalm 27:10.

"Honey, read this to me," he asked gently, putting his arm around her.

"When my father and my mother forsake me, then the Lord will take me up." The tears she had held back earlier came and we cried together, as I too held her close. The hurt and rejection Lisa had felt when Arnold left was slowly being healed. I began to take heart that even though I was again raising my daughter on my own, God would be a father to her and a husband to me. The Lord was committed to us.

Commitment. I'd never had very much of it. Within my marriages, I had given to get. But in my marriage to Jesus, God gave to me first, and kept giving regardless of how I received His love or what I did with His gifts. It was the first stable relationship I'd had. I could depend on Him. He had brought me to this church so He could work uniquely in my life through this leadership and these people. I was not there by accident. He was leading me, guiding me, and teaching me to follow after Him. When God said, "My sheep know my voice," He meant just that! I had always thought His telling me I had cancer, and the audible instruction I'd received that day on Wilshire Boulevard were rare experiences. To the contrary, I was finding out that God is constantly talking to people. I began to listen more intently. I needed to know His answers for the many question marks still facing me. I wasn't presumptuous about hearing His voice, but I waited patiently to learn from Him. If God was willing to talk to me, then I wanted to try my best to listen to Him and do what He said.

At that time, due to the tremendous growth of the church, we were very much overcrowded. Ground had just been broken for an extension to enlarge the facilities. One Wednesday evening, Jack mentioned the "big hole" that had just been dug at the side of the church. As we were meeting our costs as they arose, he indicated that funds were needed to pay for this excavation. The figure he cited was $2,000.

Sitting there listening, I felt the Lord nudge me.

"You are going to pay for that excavation," He told me.

In a savings account, I had enough money to cover the whole cost of the excavation. As I continued to ask God if this was the money He meant, I became aware of how protective I was of those funds. They represented a buffer that I didn't think I could get along without. God wanted to wean me of that dependence on material sources for my security. He wanted—for my sake—that my peace would come from Him.

As I prayed, a different figure kept coming to me. I wondered if in thinking "$1,500" I was being selfish, or cheap, or just plain scared. The day I went to the bank I was still pondering this. I didn't know until I walked up to the window how much money I was going to withdraw. When I drew out $1,500, I left feeling good about having done it, but puzzled about it.

That week, Lisa and I officially became members of The Church on the Way, and I gave my check and a letter explaining how I had been asked by the Lord to help finance the excavation.

What Jack said the next day during the service proved how exactly God had communicated to me.

"Folks," he began by trying to sound sheepish over his excitement, "I'm not such a good bookkeeper, but God is. I made a mistake last week when I told you how much the hole was going to cost. The fence around the hole cost $500, and the hole itself, $1,500."

My face quivered with the jubilance I felt and the tears that came seemed somehow pure as gold. The joy I felt stirred within me—His nearness overwhelmed me. I whispered praise in thanksgiving for His kindness. I knew in that moment that He would never leave me nor forsake me.

Lisa would be starting the new school year in a few weeks. I had not heard from Arnold in several months. The old me, indignant at his silence, wanted to file for divorce. I was impatient to get on with my life. I felt becalmed just in sight of shore. Had I really heard the Lord tell me He had a job for me? Or had I somehow missed His timing?

I wanted to be free of this frustration and turmoil. I felt I needed another viewpoint on my life, a counselor whom I could trust to look at my situation and not mince words with me. A counselor who would tell me what I needed to hear, not what I wanted to hear.

I thought about Pastor Jack. He never diluted Jesus' powerful message. The only pressure he seemed to respond to was God's directive that we be as holy as He is.

I knew God would speak through him to me. I called and made an appointment to see him.

Although he acted like he had all morning to give me, I felt that his attentive informality was just the eye of the storm. It wasn't just the atmosphere of suspended bustle, it was the evidence all around his office of the scope of his interests. Amid the many theological books, scholarly and popular, were scattered souvenirs and artifacts—a rock, sand from Israel—each invested with their own message of lessons learned. I was aware of the care he took with everything he did. I didn't want to waste his time. I sketched a picture of my marriage to Arnold and its current limbo.

"What am I going to do?" I asked finally. "I haven't the faintest notion of what Arnold wants at this point." Jack had been asking me questions here and there as I talked, clarifying his understanding of my motives and expectations. Now he spoke kindly, as if aware that I might be disappointed.

"I believe you should do just what you have been doing: wait. Don't take the initiative to begin divorce proceedings. If that is the inevitable, let your husband be the one to do it." I relaxed, satisfied with this answer.

"Yes, I see that," I said smiling. I was surprised at how calm I was, considering how I'd been feeling. My uncertainty about the future still lingered, but I felt I'd taken up enough of his time. As I prepared to take my leave, he asked me a question.

"Are you presently working?"

"No, I'm not. I suppose I should be thinking about doing something soon, but I'm waiting for the Lord to show me what." He seemed to smile at that.

"Well, we're growing so fast right now that we'll be needing to make many changes in the near future. God told us early last year to hire only people from out of the church here. I feel you are supposed to come on staff. I don't know just in what capacity we would hire you, but let's just both pray about it and I'll be in touch with you soon."

"You know, Pastor Jack, a couple of months ago the Lord told me He was going to give me a job. But never in my wildest dreams did I think it would be at The Church on the Way. I'm honored!"

"Would it be a burden on you driving the twenty miles to work and back every day?" he asked, emphasizing the more practical aspects.

"No," I breathlessly replied, "I come to Van Nuys every day! My daughter goes to a private school about five miles from here." I was getting more excited by the moment.

"How convenient of the Lord to arrange that so nicely," Jack intoned in a perfect deadpan that broke me up.

When I got home I immediately began seeking the Lord, and didn't stop until I was sure this was where He wanted me to work. Then, thrilled and a little nervous, I asked Him to make me ready for the job! Several days after our talk, Pastor Jack called.

"Could you come in tomorrow? I'd like to discuss your future on staff."

I waited apprehensively while Jack finished another appointment. When he opened the door of his office and gave me a big grin and then a bear hug, I wondered if my face was as red as the sweater he was wearing. After all, this was Pastor Jack Hayford, the man who had taught me so much, a man whom I held in awe.

As he sat behind his desk, he was casually fingering a pencil. "How would you like to be my secretary? I have a great secretary presently, but we need her talents desperately somewhere else in the church right now." He put down his pencil and looked at me as if we were making the first decision of our association. "What do you think?"

I was floored, and for a moment, speechless. Then the words tumbled out.

"Me, your secretary? Me, on staff with all of you spiritual giants? I'm so honored," I said solemnly. Then enthusiastically I said, "I'd love it!" I added pensively, "I don't know—" Jack was amused at this mixture of emotion. He tried to look concerned.

"You can do the work, can't you?" he asked with mock gravity. I heard in it a reminder that I had my own unique abilities to offer.

"Oh, yes, I'm sure of that! I'm very organized, and good at detail, and I'm a good secretary, except—" I looked sheepish, "I don't win any prizes for my typing."

"Don't worry about that. When the typing load gets too big, there are others who can help. I'll need you for more pressing matters. As far as spiritual giants are concerned, there is no such thing. Some of us have just walked with Jesus a little longer than others. You didn't see anyone here with a halo, did you?" I laughed. He continued, "I won't be in on Monday, so do you think you could start Tuesday, September 25?"

"Can you believe it? Lisa's school starts one week later than public school, and due to a Jewish holiday, it's starting one day later—September 25!"

I was reminded that in the 22nd chapter of 2 Samuel it says, "God is my strength and power: and he maketh my way perfect" (v. 33). Everything had come together beautifully to begin this new experience in my life.

"School!" Lisa was saying. "Here we go again. I wonder what this year holds for me."

As I looked through the windshield at the hot September sun rising higher in the east, I was jolted back to the present. "Interesting," I commented, "I was just wondering the same thing about myself, about what it'll be like being Pastor Jack's secretary." It boggled my mind that God had chosen me, and I wondered if I was equal to the calling.

"Good morning, and welcome to our family!" Willa, the church's receptionist, met me in the hall, her face beaming with a smile, and took my hand in warm greeting. She then introduced the woman who had just walked in; her name was Carol, Jack's secretary. I had wondered if she'd felt any resentment about the changes being made. My misgivings couldn't have been more unfounded. In Carol's cheery "Hello there," and open, kind face, I couldn't detect even a hint of regret.

We got right down to business. I asked many questions, and Carol explained some of the many functions of the senior pastor's office. All the while, other staff members were arriving and the place was alive with activity.

"I didn't know a church could be so busy, or that one man could have so much to do! Judging from the things you've been telling me, I'll have my hands full." What I didn't say was that I was wondering if I could handle it.

A certain generosity of spirit distinguished the place

from anywhere else I'd worked before. Willa had characterized it: we were a family, linked more like brothers and sisters than employers and employees. The ties were close and genuine. We were a small staff then—I was the seventeenth to come aboard—and over my three years there I watched it grow to sixty-four members. Contrary to what you'd expect in a little bureaucracy, as the size increased, so did the love. Rather than becoming impersonal, we were being stretched by the Holy Spirit to give more freely and receive more trustingly.

Like Lazarus, the grave clothes of my old ways of doing things were being unwound. I owed much to Pastor Jack for the things I learned about myself. His willingness to expose his own faults encouraged me to view myself more objectively. He seemed to have x-ray vision, and challenged our illusions about who we were. I found this out the first day.

People had always seemed to naturally take to calling me Joni, which I in turn accepted as a gesture of their ease and affection. So, innocently enough, I remarked to Pastor Jack, "You can call me Joni—everyone else does." I was startled by his frown.

" 'Joni' sounds like a little girl, and you're no longer a little girl," his eyes bored into mine. "Thanks to the healing power of Jesus, you, Joan, are the grown-up, lovely woman God created you to be. Don't settle for anything less."

This insistence was precious to me, for I knew it reflected respect for who I was. He took the time to visualize the best for me, dismantling the concepts left behind by fears, and building me up with fresh insights. "Would you believe anyone who'd lied to you as much as your fears have?"

he'd say. I understood his expectations to be a kind of tribute: when he looked at us, he saw the person God created us to be.

But at times he could be intimidating. What Jack Hayford demanded of himself, he demanded of us. And above all, he required complete integrity. Staff meetings were a revelation to me, as terrifying as they were edifying. It was impossible not to be affected by his searing indictments of his own motivations and decisions, and his gut-level repentance before God and before us. You wanted that integrity too—anything less seemed like a shadow of yourself. His humility inspired us all.

In these sessions, we did not brainstorm programs or organize drives. We sought God's direction for our church on our faces before Him. It came down to being willing to participate in God's purposes in the way He wanted them carried out. As His people, we believers were the Lord's essential collaborators, bringing His will down to earth with our prayers. How exciting it was to learn that we actually had authority over evil, and the evil one himself, Satan. As a body, we could pray and stand effectively against the forces of darkness in sickness, tragedy and wearying trials. Many times we waged spiritual warfare in those meetings, contending for God's best for the congregation, for its leadership, and for each of us present in our day-to-day lives. And how conscious I became of the bailiwick God had given to The Church on the Way in its intercessory ministry: the world.

In my role as secretary to the pastor, however, I initially struggled with feelings of inadequacy. There was no doubt in my mind that Jack was a genius. It seemed he could do anything well, even within a daily schedule that would keep three people busy for a week. One day, as I sat typing a letter, I heard the staccato machine-gun fire of his typewriter from his office, and I burst out laughing and couldn't stop. His door opened and he peered out suspiciously at me.

"I suddenly realized," I tried to explain, still giggling madly, "that you're typing twice as fast as your executive secretary!" His experession became impassive.

"Only twice?" he noted dryly.

"Well, I'm not sure you don't have a recording in there," I returned. He smiled enigmatically.

But I had my standards too, and definite ideas about the way things should be done. Working so closely with such a high-powered personality as Jack's, there were times he and I reduced each other to exasperation. Because he was my pastor, I relinquished all rights to the final word or the upper hand, sometimes only with an intense inner battle to suppress my inflamed pride. Instead of walking out with the door slamming behind me as I would have done in the past, I would mutter, "Yes, sir," and go back to work.

It began to work a healing in me. I saw I had always become hotheaded and defensive toward men in authority unless the orders they gave were on my own terms. I'm not going to let a man walk over me, I'd bristle. The love in Jack's authority pointed up the contrast between his leadership and that of the first leader in my life: my father.

My father's cruelty to my mother had destroyed my faith in him. The beatings I got at his hands humiliated me and the resentment had smoldered for years. The memories were vivid, and I knew God was giving me an opportunity to reclaim my childhood with my father. I forgave my dad, and a funny thing happened. For the first time I could ever remember, I accepted him as he was. After that, I felt like his daughter. He began to notice the difference. His feelings have been softening ever since, and not only towards me; now he is interested in getting to know God better.

"Joan," Jack said one day as he perched on the edge of my desk, "come on over to the house for lunch today. Anna and I have something to discuss with you."

It was a crisp, windy December day and that certain holiday feeling was in the air. I was looking forward to this Christmas as I had no other. I loved the new family I had in the staff, and had an inner peace that surpassed anything I'd felt before.

I thought about all the presents Arnold used to buy for us, beautiful, elaborate gifts, stacks of them, piled so high around the tree you could hardly get near it. After the excitement and the oohs and ahs, I had a strange feeling deep inside that said, Is this all there is?

But this Christmas I had Jesus, and what meaning that would give to this very special time!

"Come on in, lunch is ready and waiting." Jack's wife, Anna, greeted me with a radiant smile and a big hug. The fireplace was still flickering from an earlier fire, and the house—warm, cheery and inviting—was all dressed up for Christmas.

As I had become more closely associated with the Hayfords, I realized what a perfect balance Jack and Anna had. Her sense of humor and straightforwardness seemed to smooth out the waves created by his visionary, tenacious ways. Anna and I had become friends through the close contact my job necessitated. My secretarial duties were often lightened by a request to do some little personal errand for Anna.

"Christmas Eve is a very special time in our family," Jack was saying, "a time for just family." He paused and looked at me. "We would like you and Lisa to spend it with us. Anna and I feel you're a part of our family. You can come over directly from the service. We open our gifts and make quite a sight, everyone dancing around up to their knees in wrapping paper. Think you can handle it?" he joked.

"I'm moved to think you would want us on such a special family occasion—" I started, but I couldn't finish. Jack looked at Anna.

"I told you she would cry."

Without a husband, without a father, Lisa and I found the Hayfords to be God's gift to us that Christmas. What a grand evening! There was laughing and singing, and praising and thanking for the gift of our Father and of His Son. We exchanged gifts, and I will always cherish the precious red Bible, lovingly inscribed, and the other gift they gave that Christmas: themselves.

9

I waited months wondering what would happen to Arnold and me, and whether our marriage would survive. In the beginning I had been quite anxious, wishing I could see into the future. Then slowly I learned patience through a simple formula: wait—and wait some more.

"Hello, Joni, this is Arnold." Certainly no identification of himself was needed; his words were more like an advance warning of what was to come. "We need to talk," he said quickly, adding, "I'd like to meet you one evening this week for dinner. What about Tuesday?" I tried to control the tremor in my voice as I answered.

"I guess that's okay. Could you tell me what we're going to talk about?" I thought I knew what he had in mind.

"I'd rather not discuss it over the phone. Tell you what, I'll pick you up. How's 8:30?"

"Fine, Arnold, I'll see you then."

It seemed like it took ages for Tuesday to roll around. I

tried not to plan what I would say, and instead just asked the Lord for wisdom. "Give me your words to speak, Father—and help me to know when to keep my mouth shut!"

When I answered the door, Arnold had an edgy smile for me, and he seemed to be avoiding my eyes.

"I'd like a drink. How about you, Joni?"

I had not had anything alcoholic to drink for so long that I automatically responded, "No, thank you."

Arnold laughed tersely—or was it a sneer? "Given that up too?" There was a hint of bitterness in his voice. He knew my life had proceeded in a new direction since he left.

We talked superficially for a while between tense smiles. Finally, having never liked small talk and distrusting it now, I confronted him about the purpose of his visit. He dropped all pretense at being casual.

"I think you already know. I'd like to have a divorce. I'll be filing shortly."

After so much time apart, I had come to see his leaving as a mixed blessing. The marriage had had a strangle hold on all of us. (Its toll on Lisa I didn't discover until I saw the change in her as she came to know Jesus.) No, I wouldn't want to return to that life; it would have to be different. But now that it was about to end, I yearned for how it might have been—and could still be, with God's help. The thought occurred to me that there were other factors involved in Arnold's decision that he hadn't mentioned.

"Yes, I had suspected that's what you'd say. Have you found someone else you care for?"

"There is a girl in my life at this point. I'm in love with her. Is that what you wanted to hear?"

"I don't know what I wanted to hear. But I didn't want to hear that you're filing for a divorce. I know we had all become bitter, vengeful people, hating ourselves and one another. But I believe God could turn our marriage around, and make it something we can't conceive of right now. Much healing is needed, but if we allow the Lord to work in our lives, it could happen." But the door to Arnold's heart was already closed, and this gentle knocking only served to irritate him.

"Obviously for me to have taken this much time to decide what I wanted to do, you must know I've given it a great deal of thought. From my point of view, there is no other way," he said brusquely. I think I surprised him by offering no rebuttal. I accepted the finality of his decision calmly, hearing in it the end of my waiting.

When we went to dinner, it was as if we were old friends who had come from afar to renew their acquaintance after a long, long time. I was happy to be with him; it was important to me to be able to share with him how God had transformed my mind and emotions. Our lives were very different. He had little to say as I told him of my experiences in coming to know Jesus as the Lord of my life. As I talked, I understood more clearly that I was a new person now. Jesus had made me new.

It dawned on me that Arnold might be thinking of himself as part of my past. I wanted somehow to tell him he could be part of my present. At the door, I turned to wish him a good night.

"I will not try to stand in the way of your getting a divorce since you seem to know exactly what you want," I said gently, "but I would encourage you to give Jesus an opportunity to work in your life."

He turned, lowered his head, and slowly walking away he muttered, "I guess I don't know what the hell I want."

Two months later I was served with the divorce papers. The reality set in, but I didn't feel the guilt and anguish I had suffered in my previous divorces. I had the surpassing confidence that "There is therefore now no condemnation to them which are in Christ Jesus" (Rom. 8:1). God did not condemn me, and neither would I. But though I didn't feel God's judgment, I cared deeply for His feelings. In the Bible, it says that God hates divorce, and I only wanted to please Him. I sought Him in prayer to be able to see this event in my life from His perspective.

At the church someone gave me a copy of C.F. Lovett's book, *The Compassionate Side of Divorce*. When I read it, I felt God was showing me His attitude on divorce.

God is not a condemning person, it said. He is most sympathetic and tolerant of the divorcee, for He looks at the heart rather than the acts. When the heart is set to please God, then regardless of the acts, that person is considered perfect by God.

He went on to state that love has a higher priority than even God's own institutions: "Where the partners are changing for the worse, God does not mean for the marriage to survive at the expense of the people. Marriage was made for man, not man for marriage."

My final misgivings concerned the attitude my fellow-believers might take toward my divorce. These were laid to rest by the compassion and love I felt in their thoughts as well as their words.

Since Arnold had initiated the proceedings and was pursuing them full speed ahead, I became rather passive about it. I decided not to seek an attorney's counsel, letting Arnold arrange everything. When he presented the plan for the settlement, I was appalled. But I only said, "I want to think this over before I sign it."

Either our financial picture had changed dramatically during our separation, or something was very wrong. I began to wonder if it would not be in my best interests to at least get some legal advice before signing the agreement. I discussed this with Pastor Jack.

"Joan, since Arnold has done the filing, not you, and there seems to be quite a bit involved here, I think you should see an attorney—a Christian attorney. Let me call someone for you and set up an appointment."

So it was that I found myself in Dave's office soon after, telling him my story. There was an honesty and gentleness he had that belied his wisdom with the ways of the world. He seemed to sort out complex details effortlessly, relying on his spiritual insight as much as his legal training. I recognized he was not only a gifted lawyer, but a man of God. I saw in him the perfect mediator for my circumstances. He told me a startling fact that confirmed this.

"It's my policy not to do divorce cases any more, Joan, but I'm doing a couple right now because I was asked to by friends, just as Jack asked. Interestingly enough, they all have been doctors' wives who have had mastectomies."

As our court date approached, I began to have fears about what Arnold might try to do to me. Increasingly, God would direct me toward passages in the Bible to alleviate my fears. I was considering the consequences of a full-scale legal attack, when I opened my Bible to read,

"The fear of man bringeth a snare: but whoso putteth his trust in the Lord shall be safe" (Prov. 29:25). I remembered that the battle was God's; He was my defender, and He would see me through the days ahead.

It was a summer day and the temperature was climbing fast. Knowing it would be hot and sticky, I dreaded going downtown to court even more than I usually did. Dave was a little late. I sat watching the street come alive with cars and kids on their way to the nearby high school. I wondered how many of them were happy. Feeling sorry for yourself, Joan? I asked myself. I decided to distract myself by reading. I opened my Bible and my eyes fell to the middle of the page. The words seemed to leap up at me.

"Show me a sign for good, that those who hate me may see it, and be ashamed, because Thou, O Lord, hast helped me and comforted me" (Ps. 86:17, NAS).

What a promise! I couldn't wait to share it with Dave. I closed the Bible. Still no Dave. Then I wondered if I'd gotten the book and verse right. I couldn't recall where it was. I opened the Bible again to the same page. I understood God intended this to be a personal message; it was His assurance that He would be my comfort throughout the three years the battle was to wage.

Work became a kind of haven for me, not to escape my legal nightmare, but to renew my strength and courage to face it.

"Joan, how did it go in court yesterday?" Kathy asked. "I'm anxious to hear," she explained simply, "because I fasted and prayed for you all day."

I was flabbergasted. I didn't know Kathy well at all,

only that she was the wife of one of our elders. In a prayer circle the week before, I had explained a little about my situation, adding that I would be in court the following Tuesday and was apprehensive about going, about my attitude toward Arnold, and about the outcome of the settlement.

"Fasting! You'd do that for me? We hardly know each other!" I burst out. Kathy laughed.

"I considered it a privilege. I knew it was important to God and He asked me to do it. Don't worry, we believers get personal real fast!"

Smiling, I reported that things had gone well. "It wasn't easy, but I felt God's presence. I knew people were praying—and you just proved it!"

Kathy had just left when Pastor Darryl Roberts walked in.

"We're growing again," he announced. "Joan, this is Nancy. Nancy is to be our coordinator of volunteers. She'll be part-time for a while, probably full-time later."

"Hello!" I nodded toward a chair. "Sit down and chat with me awhile." Her hair was silvery-grey, softly curled around delicate features. Her voice was even softer. As she spoke, I felt drawn to her, and looking into her eyes I wondered what had transpired in her life to bring such sadness to their pleasant charm. She reminded me of a wounded animal.

Nancy too had been married to a physician. They had recently returned from their mission post in India and were being divorced. I commented on the similarities in our situations. As we exchanged details of our lives, the parallels became striking not only in our backgrounds, but even down to the geography. At one time we'd lived within a block of one another. Before long we were pouring out our hearts to one another, like two long-lost sisters.

"How sweet of the Lord to send you into my life right now, Nancy! My best friend and her family are moving to Santa Fe. It seems that God never closes a door until He's opened another."

"Yes, and He's so good to me! It amazes me that we're both going through the same thing right now. It gives us both someone to share with, someone who'll really understand."

God had hand-picked a friend for me, and it was the beginning of a forever kind of friendship. I watched Jesus heal her heart and supplant the hurt with His gladness. We grew together during our trials.

I knew I was in a spiritual battle as much as a legal one. I learned to rest in God's loving protection through worship and praise. The more I praised and exalted Him in the midst of my circumstances, the more assured I was that He would supply the answers to each of my problems.

I was to strongly feel the impact of being a part of the family of God all through these years. So often when I would flounder in the stress and difficulties, I felt myself borne up on the wings of the prayers of others. The love and concern of people like Kathy gave me strength during some very difficult days. It was people like Willa, whom I used to call during court recesses, and who would immediately stand with me in prayer against fear or fatigue. Consequently, my faith in God became more real to me than the sometimes vicious court proceedings.

One day in the courtroom, I heard Arnold say something about me that was completely untrue. There was an explosion within me: Of all the consummate nerve! How dare he say such a thing! The next moment I heard a soft voice inside my heart: *Faith works by love*. It dramatically recalled to me Jack's recent strong words on the subject of unforgiveness.

"The eleventh chapter of Mark says, 'Faith will not work in an unforgiving heart.' That means if you're holding anything against someone, it will hinder your faith. By harboring unforgiveness, you tie God's hands. It's a spiritual law as Jesus said, 'If you do not forgive, then the Father cannot forgive you.' "

I felt wronged and hurt. But I knew that in God's scheme of things, I shouldn't rely on feelings. Forgiveness is an act of the will. I responded, "Father, forgive me for those thoughts. Forgive Arnold for the lie; and help me to love him anyway." The bitterness dissipated.

There were other instances of my character being maligned before the court. But I found I'd rather have a clean heart before God than a clear reputation before all the tribunals of the world.

It was the day of our last session. I was sitting in court, absorbed in my thoughts, the activity around me just a blur. The finality of the moment loomed so large, seeming to bring the past into focus. Had I once had a lax attitude toward divorce? It was never easy, true, but neither had it ever been this difficult. I felt regret welling up inside me as once more I asked God's forgiveness for not treating His gift of marriage with more care. Oh, I had always thought

I'd taken my marriages seriously. But now I realized how shallow they had been.

"We'll be ready for summation in a few minutes." The judge's words jolted me out of my reverie. He turned to Arnold..

"Are you satisfied there are no grounds for reconciliation? Do you want this divorce granted?" The floor seemed to drop away from my feet.

"Yes," Arnold answered. I began to cry. I was thinking back to a day long ago.

It was a few days after Arnold and I had returned from our honeymoon. I was quite a rose gardener, and took great pride in the show-quality varieties I grew. Arnold had stepped out early in the morning, cut one of my lovely roses, and brought it, still wet with dew, to me.

"For my lovely lady!"

"You didn't cut it at the proper place," was my reply. I then lectured him on how to cut a rose. Arnold never knew about the pangs of remorse I experienced over this episode. Now, in the courtroom, I saw how something must have died in Arnold each time I failed to fully appreciate his efforts to please me.

All my justifications fell away, and I felt deluged by guilt as my past sins stood out in ugly relief. I had no defense. "Oh, God—!" was all I could manage in my horror.

Suddenly I felt as though strong arms were holding me close. I knew they were the Lord's. He didn't care about those old rationalizations, now only tears evaporating in a Los Angeles courtroom. He cared about one thing: that I would accept the forgiveness He had offered me, the forgiveness that would make me whole. His Son had died so that my heart didn't have to be rent in pieces through failure and defeat. God showed me then why this divorce was like none of the others. I had discovered the faith I needed to believe He could redeem what I had so carelessly thrown away—my marriage.

Lord, I cared too late! I cried out soundlessly. I looked at Arnold, and saw the Arnold I had married, Arnold of the sweet and sensitive nature, the Arnold I had loved.

"Lord," I whispered, "make him new again, make him beloved to you." Maybe now I was right on time.

It was raining. Unusual for late April in California. Through the windows of my home, I watched the branches of a row of birch trees sway in a soft breeze that was blowing from the nearby hills.

I was going to miss this house—these beautiful green hills looking like a run of velvet. The smell of horses on the breeze. My huge rose garden. The fresh air and blue sky. I could no longer afford to keep such an expensive house, and I needed a breathing spell to make a new home for Lisa, a place of refreshing and preparation for our future. I knew it was time for a big change.

"Jack, I need to talk to you today; right now if possible, before I change my mind."

"Sounds serious. Judging from the look on your face, I vote for now. Come into my office." I had barely sat down before I blurted out my message.

"I'm leaving."

"For the day, or forever?" Jack was smiling, but I was crying.

"It's been such a difficult decision to make, but I believe I should try to sell my house myself, or at least be at home taking care of things while it's being sold. I want to take time to decide where to relocate; and I'd like to rest for a few months before going on with whatever God has for me." The words were rushing out and I wondered if they made any sense.

"Don't ever leave me, Joan. I've told you before, don't ever leave me!"

This little saying of Jack's had become a joke between us. But Jack saw it only pained me now. He became serious.

"The Lord showed me a few months ago that you would be leaving. I've been preparing myself for this." I felt reassured that I had indeed heard the Lord, and so I ventured out further.

"I believe I know who is to be my replacement: Janet."

"I believe the Lord showed me that too," was his reply. "Several months ago I had the distinct feeling she'd one day be working for me instead of Dick. I didn't have the details, but you did—as usual," he added with a grin.

As my last day approached, how difficult my leaving became for me. So many friends, so many people I loved, people I was used to seeing and sharing with every day. I was going to miss them. Lisa and I had chosen a house, not yet built, about eight miles further west of where we lived now, and I wondered if I would be so far away as to be forgotten. And there was my involvement in bringing the vital hope and transforming faith in God's Word, and in His Son, Jesus. I was going to miss a lot of things.

When I walked into my office on that last day on staff,

166

Jack intercepted me before I got to work.

"I don't want you to work today. By the time a few people step in here to say good-by you won't be fit to work anyway!" Then he brought a beautiful corsage from behind his back and pinned it on me. "Joan, people really love you here, and they may have some difficulty saying good-by, so be prepared for a long day!"

We all met as usual for the staff morning prayer time in the large room downstairs. The place was a beehive of activity with the preparations for a luncheon—for me. Nancy was crying and I couldn't look at her, being on the verge of runaway tears myself.

After our time of prayer, Jack announced that there would be a general disruption of all office routines that day as I went from office to office saying good-by. He turned out to be exactly right: there was much hugging and kissing and crying on staff that day. I saw the true *agape* love that people are capable of when they suffer, grow and rejoice together. When I came back to my desk just before lunch, there was an envelope propped up on my typewriter simply addressed, "Joan." I recognized Jack's stationery and slowly broke the seal.

Dear Joan:

Although words seem wooden at a time like this, I felt the desire to put into a more permanent form a brief expression of my thanksgiving to the Lord for your work with me these three years.

It was Esther of whom it was written that she rose to influence "at such a time as this." The emphasis is on her timely appearance and personal preparation for a God-ordained mission at a distinct period in Israel's history.

On looking back, that's how I see your coming to this office.

There is no way to describe the release and relief you brought. This is no commentary on your predecessor, but simply an acknowledgment that a new time had come and a specifically gifted person was needed.

The way you have been that person is a matter of record now. You have fulfilled your calling, my sister; and it is my privilege as your brother, your pastor and your boss to commend you in Jesus' name.

There is a certain dignity that you have brought to my office, and for that matter, to the staff as a whole, that no one else could bring. In a very positive way, the operations of our staff and of my office in particular, will never be the same because of the contributions you made.

I know you well enough to know that you will have difficulty believing your work actually accomplished the kind of things I am crediting you with, but it is nonetheless true. You have been a jewel and a joy, and Anna and I couldn't love you any more than we do, nor will we any less in the days to come.

Very thankful for you,
Jack

As I sat at the beautifully catered luncheon given in my honor, fingering the lovely necklace of three intertwined gold hearts that represented my ties with these people, I thought of Esther.

To be compared with Esther was a startling tribute—she was a great woman of God. And yet, as I looked around at these dedicated, loving people, I knew that wherever there are hearts open to Jesus, there will be Esthers. Every believer willing to say yes to God will rise at their special hour and shine over the land God gives them. In His kingdom, He gives us each a destiny, shaping and refining us to be what we were meant to be.

Epilogue

When I began to write this book, I did not plan to tell all. Parts of my life—it seemed to me—were too shameful to disclose, especially in a published book. My marriage to Bill and my common-law relationship with Keith were the two chief skeletons. Nobody's business but mine, I concluded.

When I was in the midst of writing this book, I had my semiannual physical examination. Dr. Marks told me then that, six years after my mastectomy, I was "one healed lady."

By the time I was nearly finished writing this book, both of these situations had changed considerably. Let me tell you what happened.

Dennis Baker and I were discussing the book over dinner one night in Westwood. He had recently agreed to work with me on the writing of the book, and was probing me about some vague points in the story. He said he was trying to get the chronology straight in his mind.

"Now, exactly how many years were you married to Keith?" he asked.

"Well, the truth is, we weren't actually married, you see."

"I see." He was obviously waiting for me to go on.

"We lived together for six years before I left him for Arnold. But I don't want to get into that in the book. It's painful enough to have to tell you about, why should I tell the whole world?"

His brow furrowed ever so slightly, and I stiffened. But he seemed to relax. "Joan, just pray about it."

"Okay."

And I did. Soon I saw how dishonest the book would become if I omitted the truth about my relationships with these two men. But, I reasoned, if I told about them now, after having concealed them for so long, it could prove embarrassing to some people who were very important to me—especially my family and my pastor. What would they think? All of them would be in the book with me.

I concluded that the only thing to do was to go to them, tell them the truth, and see what they would say.

Shortly after that, I arranged to meet with Jack Hayford at his home one evening. Anxiety and eagerness trod hand in hand across my mind as the appointment drew near.

"Hi, dear one!" Jack gave me a big hug. We chatted a few minutes with some of the other members of his family. Then he said, "I understand you want to talk to me about something."

"Yes, but it'll require privacy."

"Fine, let's use the den."

Jack beckoned me to the couch and sat down across

from me in the rocker.

"Jack, this is going to be kinda like 'true confessions.' I hope you'll still love me when I'm finished."

He laughed good-heartedly, "Let's hear it."

"I accepted the job as your secretary without telling you all the truth about myself." My face reddened with shame, but I plunged into my story—mostly about Bill and Keith. Jack sat silently throughout my recitation. I was weeping as I finished, "Jack, will you forgive me?"

"Of course I forgive you, Joan. Actually, I feel a sense of pride right now. Jesus has brought you a long way for you to be willing to be this transparent. I'm proud to be your pastor. What you've just done shows me the extreme sensitivity I saw in you at certain times. I had no way of knowing the depth of your hurt, but I could often perceive its effects."

"Thanks so much, Jack. But I still want you to have the right to censor anything in the book you want to."

"Joan, don't worry about it. It's not going to be necessary. Have you told Lisa yet?"

"No, I haven't. I intend to speak with her next."

"Good. I'm so pleased you came. And you know I still love you, don't you?"

"Yes, I really do. Oh, the relief to be myself without anything to hide!"

Jack hugged me again and then I was on my way to tell Lisa. Telling her is going to be more difficult, I thought. What will she think of her own mother having done such things? Would she ever trust me again?

"'Honey, come sit down. I have something to tell you. It's not going to be easy, and when I'm done, please be honest about your feelings, okay?"

"Okay, mom, but what on earth is it? Sounds pretty serious."

She was right, but I had to trust God. I plunged once again into my story. Her eyes were wide with astonishment by the time I finished. She managed a feeble smile.

"I'm glad you told me, mom."

"Can you forgive me, darling?"

"I don't feel I have anything to forgive you for. But if you need to hear me say it, then yes!"

As with Jack, I told her I would leave out of the book anything she might object to. She chose not to exercise that option. I was grateful.

The following week, I told my brother and his wife, Carole, my dad and stepmother, Lenora, and Aunt Faith and Uncle Bob. Everyone was wonderful and took Lisa's stance. They didn't feel there was anything to forgive.

"Hon, it was your life and your business," my dad sweetly said. "Anyway, for one reason or another, we've all done things we later wish we hadn't."

It had been painful, but in the process of confession, the Lord worked a new healing in me. The power of those hidden things was broken, and I was freer than ever before.

On Memorial Day, 1978, I was busily working on the manuscript for this book. I was writing about how God had revealed to me I had cancer, and how that eventually led to surgery in the nick of time. That same evening I noticed a small nodule just under my right arm on the lateral portion of my chest wall. Now what could this be, I wondered. I called Dr. Marks on Thursday. He asked me to come to his office that afternoon.

"I don't think it's anything to worry about, Joni. It's movable and that's a good sign. Probably just a granulated stitch from the old surgery. But to be certain, I want to take it out tomorrow morning. Okay?"

"What can I say? Let's get it over with."

Neither Lisa nor I said much on the way to the hospital that morning. To say the least, I was apprehensive. Dr. Marks was only going to use a local anesthetic. That would be a first for me, and I dreaded the possibility of pain.

I was prepped and taken to the operating room. Dick was waiting there for me.

"We're not going to make too much out of this, Joni. We'll just get that thing out of there and let you go home as soon as the frozen section is done."

The surgery didn't take very long, and I was wheeled into the recovery room to await the pathology report. I was confident, as was Dick, that everything would be fine. As I lay there, I quietly, trustfully praised God. Dick approached my bed. I had seen that look on his face before and I tensed.

"Joni, I can't believe it—that darn thing was malignant. You have a recurrence of breast cancer. After all this time, I don't understand it—I was sure you were healed."

I was crying hard. "Dear God, how can this be happening again? Dick, why, why?"

"Joni, you're asking me something I can't answer." He ordered a tranquilizer for me and then asked, "Where's Lisa? I want to tell her first."

"She's in the waiting room down the hall." Dick went out to talk to her and I prayed, "God, please help her now—give her strength, help her to lean on you."

A nurse arrived with my medication. She took my hand,

her eyes filled with compassion. "I'm so sorry. I wish I could help you."

"Thank you for being so sweet," I answered. "But only God can help me now. He got me through this once before and I know He will again. The Bible says, 'I will restore health unto thee, and I will heal thee of thy wounds' " (Jer. 30:17).

"I admire your faith, Mrs. Harper. Somehow, I believe you."

I wished my faith were a more constant thing, carrying me breezily through events like these. But, as usual, it was a struggle.

I knew enough about cancer to understand that my case was serious. Very few cancer victims survive their second bout with the disease. So here I was, facing death again. A feeling of helplessness swept over me. Life—my life—seemed so frail.

I went back and forth in my mind. Nothing I might do, I thought, would really alter the course of this deadly disease. Then I thought of God. I could turn to Him. I could plead for my life. He seemed so silent. I felt angry. There was so much to live for, and I was being cut off—isolated from the normal course of life in which people have a future.

Horror gripped me until I began to resist it. The malignancy might destroy some of my body, but it couldn't destroy me. I was still me. Somehow that affirmation began to take root in my mind. It would help me in the coming days as the struggle continued.

Lisa walked into the room. She came over and put her arms around me. We held one another tightly. Both of us were crying.

But after a few moments, she pulled away and went to the nurses' station, where she asked to use the phone. She called the church.

"Willa, I know you guys have been praying all morning, but don't stop now. Mom has cancer again." I suddenly saw her as a maturing young woman. She was handling herself well—doing the right thing. I was pleased and perplexed. Did she need me any longer? Did anyone really need me?

There it was: was I willing to just be me without being needed? I would have to decide.

Lisa walked back to my bedside and held my hand until it was time to go.

Shortly after I got home, John Farmer and Dick Robertson—two of the pastors from the church—came out to pray for me and anoint me with oil for healing. It was a powerful time, and I sensed the Lord telling me during it that I would be all right.

That evening, Nancy, her daughter Janet, and two of our pastors' wives, Teresa Robertson and Carolyn Ross, came out to pray with me. They wonderfully encouraged me. Dennis Baker arrived shortly after they did. I think we were all amazed at the light, cheerful tone of the evening. God is so good.

The following week I was admitted to the hospital for three days of scans and tests. Each day I was quite busy, and each evening my faithful friends visited. We had whopping good times. We prayed, talked and laughed. One evening they had to ask us to quiet down a little. The evening that happened, one of the nurses told me, "Usually in situations like this, the patient and visitors are glum, but you have a party in here every evening. We all talk about how radiant you look, down at the nurses' station."

"That's because of the Lord Jesus!" I grinned broadly. "I'm putting my trust in Him."

I was delighted for the opportunity to say it. And there were other opportunities to talk about Jesus while I was there. A nurse who goes to my church was working on that floor one day, and introduced me to another patient, a young woman who didn't know Jesus is the Healer. She was so ready to listen.

In the evenings, after everyone had left and the laughter had faded, I was alone with my thoughts. Sleep did not come easily, and I used the time to pray. By the third night of this, I began to get a glimmer of God's glory. It was awesome and lovely—and I was utterly dependent on Him. I began to see it. When I could honestly say, "Lord, you alone are all my joy," then everything would fall into place. I was getting close to that joy.

Dr. Marks and Dr. Bluming, the oncologist, both helped keep my spirits up. They were positive about my condition, and I looked forward to their smiling faces early each morning.

The morning I was to be discharged, Dick Marks walked in with a bright, "Got good news for you, Joni. That thing is localized to the chest wall. All of the other tests were negative. Things are looking good!"

Then he became serious and looked at me uneasily. "I cannot tell you how hard this has hit me. That it has happened to you makes it very personal for me. I've been through a lot with you—and now this. It's forced me to completely reevaluate things." Then he reached over and touched my Bible on the bedstand. "That fellow hasn't given us all the answers."

My eyes were misting. Dick continued, "I used to think surgery was *the* answer. That's one of the reasons I became a surgeon. But surgery isn't the answer. Your case is a perfect example. We're making progress but we've got a long way to go. I don't have the answers. I don't have the answers."

"Oh, Dick, God bless you. It's refreshing to hear you speak like that. Want to know something? It reassures me that you feel that way. Only God is omnipotent, and I'd feel nervous around a physician who regarded himself as omnipotent."

Back home, Lisa was helpful and considerate—for a couple of days. Then I began to notice that she seemed angry with me. What was this? I was hurt and bewildered, until the light dawned. Our relationship had been close, almost exclusive. Suddenly she was faced with the possibility I might not be around much longer.

"Lisa, your attitude has been less than loving the last few days, and I think I know why. You're afraid—afraid I'm going to die and leave you alone. Well, I'll tell you something. I'm afraid, too." Lisa's eyes brimmed with tears. "Honey, we've got to lick this thing together. I need you right now, I need your love, Lisa. Please don't shut me out. I don't want to go through this all alone."

"I'm sorry, mom. I am scared. But God will help us through this just like He did the last time. We're in a spiritual battle, aren't we?"

"Yes, and we're going to fight. I'm not going to let some devil dupe me into giving up and going into despair. I don't intend to die one day before God's appointed time."

Joan, the giver, has had to become Joan, the receiver. I will never know how many people have prayed for me. Willa told me one day that I would never know how many people have fasted for me. I had just told her that my brother and his wife had gone on a three-day fast after receiving the news that I had cancer again.

I have felt as though I were in a protected place, like an incubator—warm and safe inside while the storm rages without. My hopes are high; they must be a gift from God.

I hope for many things. I hope for permanent recession of the cancer. I hope for the chance to grow and change and develop my personal potential. And I hope for a future with the people I love in a way that perhaps can be fully understood only by those who have tasted their own mortality.

But I hope in only one thing, and it transcends time and the topography of a life:

Our God reigns.

For free information on how to receive
the international magazine

LOGOS JOURNAL

also Book Catalog

Write: Information - LOGOS JOURNAL CATALOG
Box 191
Plainfield, NJ 07061

**We will be please to provide
locations of bookstores in your
area selling Logos titles.**

Call: (201) 754-0745

Ask for bookstore information service